RAINY DAY FUN AND GAMES

Maureen Maddren

Illustrated by Mike Scott

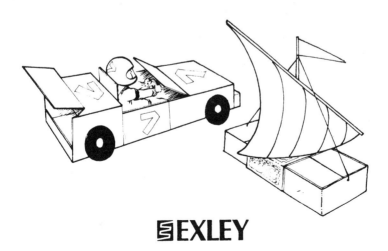

EXLEY

Published in Great Britain in 1989 by Exlkey Publications Ltd,
16 Chalk Hill, Watford, Herts WD1 4BN, United Kingdom.

British Library Cataloguing in Publication Data
Maddren, Maureen.
 Rainy day fun and games.
 1. Activities for children – For children.
 I. Title.
 II. Scott, Mike.
 790.1'922

ISBN 1-85015-186-5 (h/b)
ISBN 1-85015-187-3 (p/b)

Art Director: Nick Maddren.
Typeset by Brush Off Studios, St Albans, Herts AL3 4PH.
Printed and bound in Hungary.

Introduction

Do you dread rainy days that keep you inside when you long to go out and play? We just know this book will change all that. It's got over 90 fun ideas for things to make and do. There are twelve chapters, all with bright suggestions for ways of spending a rainy day in an enjoyable way.

There are quiet games and noisy games, models to construct, presents to make, plants to grow and magic to perform. You'll learn how to do new crafts as well as make toys that will fascinate your friends with their ingenuity. And you can spend time in the kitchen making delicious things to eat.

There is amusement here for everyone. Whatever your mood, you will find something of interest; perhaps take up a new hobby or start a new collection. The last chapter even gives you ideas for planning for future rainy days so that you'll positively look forward to the next dark cloud that comes along!

Contents

Chapter 1
Dressing up 9
In days of old ... 10
They came from outer space 12
If you go down in the woods today ... 14
Shiver me timbers! 16

Chapter 2
Let's pretend 17
Using the table 18
Flights of fantasy 20
Box cars 22
Box boats 23
Flying carpet 24

Chapter 3
Playing with toys 25
Put your cars on the road! 26
Zoo time 27
Land of the dinosaurs 28
Using your marbles 30
Grand prix 32
Horse trials 33
Down on the farm 34

Chapter 4
Cooking is fun! 35
Dainty delights 36
Scrumptious salads 38
Simple pizzas 39
Oaty things 40
Pastry things 42

Chapter 5
Party games 43
In the rush hour 44
Pin the tail on the donkey 44
Treasure Trail 45
Stampede 45
Can you draw me? 46
Querky quoits 46
Relay race 47
Musical statues 47
What is it? 48
What a smell! 48
Tiddlywink obstacle course 49
Beetle 49
How nosey! 50
Chin-chin! 50

Chapter 6

Card and board games 51

Snakes and ladders 52
Shove ha'penny 53
Tiddlywink birds 54
Dominoes 55
Matching pairs 56
Snap 56
Old maid 57
My ship sails 58

Chapter 7

Entertain your friends 59

Pump up the volume 60
Doh-ray-me 61
Telepathy 62
Black magic 63
Clever paper-clips 64
Magic matchbox 65
Playing with puppets 66
Puppet show 68

Chapter 8

The appliance of science 69

Turning white flowers blue 70
Water magnifying glass 71
Bush telephone 71
Whizz bang 72
Magic fountain 73
Messing about in boats 74
Launch the shuttle 75
Grow your own crystals 76
Stalagmites and stalactites 77
Indoor lightning 78

Chapter 9

Before your very eyes 79

Peep shows 80
Tops and whizzers 82
Now you see it ... 84
... now you don't 85
Zoetrope 86
Flicker books 87
The "turning wonder" 88

Chapter 10
Creative crafts 89
Seed and pasta pictures 90
Don't just eat it, wear it! 91
Rolled paperwork 92
Paper flowers 93
3-D pictures 94
Noah's ark 95
Shoe-box dolls' house 96
Dolls' house furniture 97
Not bookmarks again! 98

Chapter 11
Grow it indoors 99
A topping garden 100
The miniature garden 101
Growing things to eat 102
Growing plants from cuttings 103
Plants from stones and seeds 104
A garden in a jar 106
Cacti 107
Winter flowers 108

Chapter 12
Preparing for a rainy day 109
Collecting for an album 110
Recycling greetings cards 111
Using pressed flowers 112
Collages 114
Mosaic pictures 115
Things with shells 116

Bibliography
Berry's Book of Cunning Contraptions, *Roland Berry* (Puffin 1977)
The Book of Games and Pastimes, *Steward Cowley* (Deans International Publishing 1986)
Growing Plants at Home, *Althea* (Dinosaur Publications)
Growing Things, *Elizabeth Gundry* (Piccolo 1973)
Making Things Grandma Made, *Marjorie Stapleton* (Studio Vista 1975)
Regency and Victorian Crafts, *Jane Toller* (Ward Lock 1969)
Victorian Kinetic Toys, *Philip and Caroline Freeman Sayer* (Evans Brothers Ltd 1977)

1 Dressing Up

Dressing up is fun, so don't let any of your family *ever* throw anything away. Persuade them that a dressing-up box will keep you quiet for hours and hours – that usually wins them over.

You can't really be an alien or a medieval knight or lady if you don't look the part. But you don't want to spend ages making a costume either, so the answer is to have a really good dressing-up box with old clothes, sheets, curtains and hats that can swiftly and magically be adapted to suit the character you want to be.

The next few pages show you how you can dress ready to be transported back to the Middle Ages, or forward in time to be an alien. You can frolic as a woodland creature or swashbuckle as a pirate. Then you can invent more characters of your own.

In days of old ...

... when knights were bold (well, some of them probably were). If you feel like doing some dragon-slaying or rescuing distressed maidens, then your costume is quite easy. Dive into the dressing-up box and find an old pair of ski pants. If there's a blouse there with full sleeves, use that, too. Then you need a belt for your waist and a jaunty hat. A feather would look good stuck in it, but if you can't find a real one, make one out of paper. Draw a curly feather shape, cut it out and make little slits along it to give it a feathered edge.

If you want to be a knight then you need some large cardboard boxes. Cut out two person-shaped body pieces and tie them loosely together with string. Then, with a felt-tipped pen, draw on the chain-mail links. Your sword can also be made out of cardboard. You may need some help with cutting the cardboard as it's usually very thick.

Or you could try your hand at making one of the costumes shown here. They are really very simple and most are based on clothes you may already have in your dressing-up box.

The tunics worn by the king, peasant and knight are all made from two straight pieces of material, stitched at the sides and shoulders, and big enough to slip easily over the head. Tie a belt around the middle and you have the basic costume.

The king will need a cardboard crown, decorated with glitter and sequins, a cloak and some jewels. The peasant's hood is made from a long piece of material which narrows to a point at one end. Join the edges together leaving a gap in the middle for the face. The shoulder edges can be cut into a pattern as shown. Our knight appears to have a saucepan on his head, but you could make something similar out of cardboard.

The costumes of the monk and the lady are both based on similar designs. Two full-length T-shaped pieces of material are stitched together leaving, of course, the sleeve ends and the neck open! The monk's hood is made from one long piece of material stitched around two sides, leaving a large space at the front of the hood for the face. The lady needs a little cape collar and a length of material wound over the top of her head and under her chin. The head-dress is simply a band of stiff material or cardboard to which is stuck or sewn some soft material that will hang in loose folds.

They came from outer space

Your spaceship lands. The door opens and you step out to meet these strange earth creatures. They look so different, but you have come in peace to tell them more about your planet – what it's like, who lives there, what you eat and drink, and how you like to spend your free time.

But are you dressed the part? No one will believe you're from another planet dressed in jeans and a tee-shirt so here's what you do.

Take two large sheets of cardboard – the bottoms of two cardboard boxes will do. Join them with straps on the shoulders and at waist level. Then add foil or bottle top knobs and draw in a control panel or two to make you look fully computerized. Make a mask and draw an enormous eye in the middle, attach two sticks to either side with lumps of model clay on the tops to represent aerials or antennae. Wear gardening gloves and make thick pads out of material or newspapers to tie around your knees. A nice touch would be to have flippers or a pair of gloves on your feet. This will make you walk quite differently to the way you usually get about.

Another alien could have a costume based on a clean polythene sack. Cut armholes and a headhole in it so that it slips on easily. *Don't put the bag on without cutting the holes in it first as polythene can cling to the face and cause suffocation.* Tie a belt around the waist and stick foil tops or large foil circles down the front. Make a big collar out of two semi-circular pieces of paper and tie them together on the shoulders with wool or string. This alien should have some really big boots on its feet and a couple of large box ears.

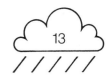

These can be made from any small boxes found in the kitchen. Just cut a long slit in one side and hook them over your ears.

Now you're ready to meet the earthlings.

The exciting thing about dressing as an alien is that you don't have to follow any particular pattern or design. You can plan your own costume depending on what materials you have to hand. If you have a dressing-up box, sort through it to see what you can re-use.

Pad out the sleeves of an old pullover, cut a slit just behind the sleeves in the back of the pullover for your arms to go through and stitch gloves to the ends of the sleeves. Put it on and you will instantly become a four-armed alien with that extra pair of hands that you have always wanted!

If you go down in the woods today ...

... you could meet cats, mice, owls, dogs, pigs and rabbits. Well, perhaps not pigs, unless they were visiting, of course.

These masks would be fun to make for a birthday party with an animal theme. You could give all the guests a mask and have a woodland picnic. They are very easy to make. Measure your face from top of head to tip of chin and cut out a piece of thick paper or thin white cardboard of the right length. It needs to be wide enough to go around your face from ear to ear. Stick a length of elastic to your mask so that it stretches comfortably around the back of your head.

Now you can add the detail to the faces, making sure you put the eyes and nose in the right places so that you can see and breathe! The ears are slightly different for each animal and these can be stuck on the back of the mask or slotted over the mask, as shown.

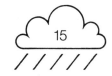

Put in lots of detail to make your masks look really effective. Draw in some nice big whiskers on the cat, mouse and rabbit. Give the mouse pink ears and the dog a bright red tongue. The owl would probably like some feathers and the pig should have pink ears and a pink snout, or he could be pink all over.

Look through some books on farm animals, pets and wild animals to see what other masks you could make.

You can make masks like these for any kind of fancy dress, from space monsters to witches and wizards. It is useful to know how to do them, particularly if you are in a carnival procession and your club leader or teacher says, "Now, how shall we make our masks?" You can shoot your hand up and tell everyone.

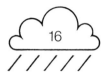
Shiver me timbers!

Playing at being pirates is even more fun if you've got some real treasure to find. Perhaps you could persuade a member of your family to hide some "treasure" for you and draw a map giving you clues as to where it's hidden. While he or she is doing this, you can rummage in your dressing-up box. Find an old pair of trousers and roll them up to just below the knee – or you could use the ones you're wearing – then wear boots or sandals on your feet. An old shirt will do for your top half – the more ragged the better. You could make a pirate's hat like the one in the picture by cutting out two identical shapes from stiff paper and joining them on the inside with two narrow strips of paper so that the hat sits comfortably on top of your head.

Another sort of pirate headgear can be made by using a square scarf. Fold it in half diagonally and put it on your head so that the long edge comes halfway down your forehead. Then tie the two ends in a knot at the back of your head.

With an inflatable parrot on your shoulder and a cardboard cutlass in your hand you're ready to find the hidden treasure.

2 Let's pretend

Some of the best games are "pretend" ones when you make up a
story and act it out. They usually start by someone saying , "I know,
let's pretend to be motor racing drivers," or "Let's pretend we're
going off in a spaceship to discover an unknown planet." It's a lot
more fun, too, if you've a few "props". All you really need are two
or three cardboard boxes, as you'll see in the next few pages.

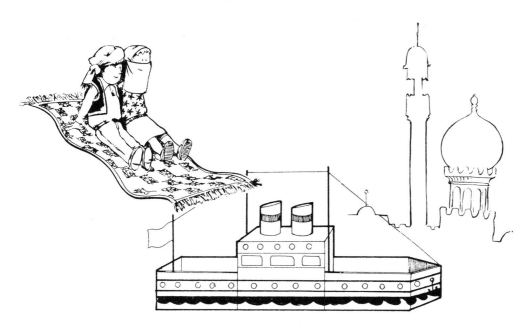

Using the table

Your dining room table makes a very good starting point for lots of different games. With the addition of some cardboard or sheets or blankets you can quickly change its appearance.

It can be a cave. Drape a large sheet over the whole table and pin or tie one side up to form an entrance. Then pile some smaller boxes around the entrance. Perhaps you would be allowed to stand some pot plants around it to give it a "natural" look. Now you can be cave dwellers, hunting for food during the day and keeping wild animals at bay during the night.

Then your table can become a cottage. Drape a sheet over three sides. Open out a cardboard box, or stick several pieces of cardboard together with parcel tape. Draw some windows and a door onto it. Cut around one long side and the top of the door and bend the other side back so that your door will open and shut.

Use the same idea to make a space capsule or a castle. You can again drape a sheet over three sides and just make a front or, if you're feeling really keen, you can make all four sides out of cardboard and join them together at the corners with parcel tape.

The spaceship door will lift up, so cut along the two long sides only. The castle has a drawbridge which you can raise and lower by attaching string to the top two corners, then thread the other end of the string through holes just above the doorway as shown.

You will need some help cutting and folding all these boxes so make sure there is someone around who has some free time to lend a hand before you begin work.

Flights of fantasy

Biplane

Who'd have thought cardboard boxes could be so exciting? Pick up some nice big, roomy ones from your supermarket. Try to get several of the same size, then you can turn them into all sorts of wonderful machines.

This biplane was made using just five boxes: one to sit in, one each for the wings, one for the tail and one for the navigator's seat (behind the pilot). Join the boxes together with strips of strong parcel tape.

Cut out four propeller blades from some cardboard and attach these to a stick. Push the stick through the front of the plane then you can sit in the pilot's seat and make the propeller go round! To make your plane look even more realistic, draw some nice, big identification initials on the wings, side and tail.

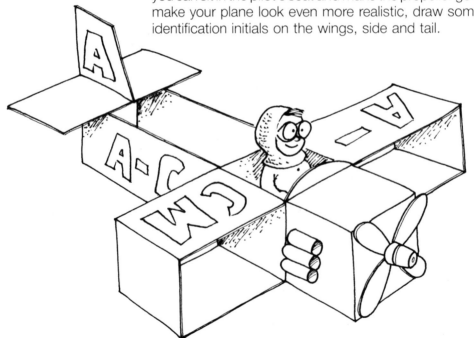

Spacecraft

For this spacecraft you need three boxes taped together, one behind
the other. Ask a grown-up to trim the first box so that your spacecraft
can have a pointed nosecone.

Take a fourth box and cut three windows in it, then, when you
climb into the middle compartment of your spacecraft this box will
become the cockpit hood. Now you can start to put the detail on.
Open out two of the top flaps of the box at the back of your craft
and taper them to make a tail fin. Then tape cardboard tubes or
rolled up newspapers to front, sides and back to act as rocket
boosters. You could even cover some of these in foil.

Your spacecraft is now complete, so ...
5, 4, 3, 2, 1, lift off!

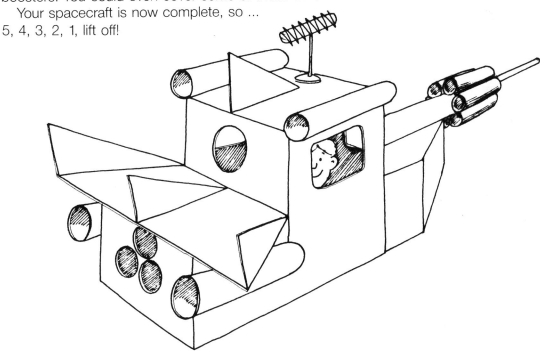

Box Cars

"And here comes number 7, roaring around the track, but number 11 isn't far behind, can he catch him?"

Well, it will surprise everyone if he does, as these cars don't have engines!

You need three square cardboard boxes. Join them together with parcel tape, sticking all the flaps of the middle one down inside the box for extra strength. Cut around one side of the end box so that this piece of cardboard can be bent to slope up, as shown, and will form the rear spoiler. Cut out four circles for the wheels and another one for the steering wheel. Look for a garden cane, about 60 cm (2 ft) long as this will make a good steering column. Fix your wheel to one end of it and push the other end through the cardboard so that it disappears into the front box. With paint or felt-tipped pens, draw in the car's number and put in details like lights, radiator and door handles.

You can make a family car in a similar way, but this time you need two large oblong boxes, stuck firmly together with sticky tape. Make the wheels and steering wheel as before and put cushions in the back for your passengers to sit on.

You are now ready for a trip to the sea, to the country, or, if you are feeling really adventurous, why not try an African safari? Pack your camera, tents and food and off you go into the bush looking for wild animals.

Box Boats

You can choose to make either a stately liner for a trip around the world or a smaller sailing boat for skimming along the river.

Pick up two large square boxes from your local supermarket and ask someone to cut around one so that you have two equal halves. Stick all flaps down with parcel tape so that your liner doesn't break up in mid-ocean. Make the other box into a cube by sticking all the flaps together so that they cannot open. This is the middle section of the liner and should be attached to the other two box halves with strong parcel tape. Try to find some cardboard tubes for funnels and stick these on top of the middle section. Then draw portholes along both sides.

Your liner is now ready to sail, with either you inside it or a boatload of toys, ready to set off for the cruise of a lifetime.

To make a sailing boat, both boxes should be open with all flaps taped down securely inside. Make a cardboard rudder, like the one in the picture, and then tackle the sail. You will need a pole about 1.5 m (5 ft) long attached to the middle section of the boat. Then ask for an old sheet or piece of material and cut a triangular shape from it. Attach it to the mast and front and back (bow and stern) of the boat as shown.

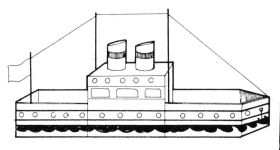

Flying carpet

A flying carpet is so easy to make – you just need a piece of carpet large enough for you and your friends to sit on. If your family doesn't have any spare pieces of carpet lying around then you'll have to make do with a flying sheet or flying leftover-piece-of-material. They work just as well.

You can then command your magic carpet to go anywhere you want – Egypt to see the pyramids, India to see the Taj Mahal and fabulous palaces, Antarctica to see the penguins, Australia to see the kangaroos. You could make flat cut-out models of these places and things and stand them up around the room. Then, when your carpet lands, go off and explore each country in turn to see what wonders it has to offer.

When you've been to all the countries you want to see, take a trip back in time to find the dinosaurs, the Romans or the Vikings. Take a Roman back to your own time and show him all the amazing things we have now. He'll know about central heating because he had that, but he won't know about television, radio and computers.

After that, fly off to outer space, explore the planets, meet some space creatures and see how they live. Then drop in on the moon on your way home.

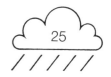
3 Playing with toys

Here's a chapter packed full of ideas for playing with your toys. For instance, if you have lots of cars, why not make a road layout? Perhaps you have herds of animals that have nowhere to go – so make a zoo or safari park. With a little imagination – and a lot of cardboard – you can make almost anything, from a landscape for your dinosaurs to live in to a motor-racing circuit for your Formula One cars.

Put your cars on the road!

With this road layout you can have traffic jams, roadworks, carnival processions and perhaps learn some road signs at the same time.

First of all you need our old friend, a large sheet of cardboard. It doesn't have to be square so if you open out a cardboard box you will have lots of interesting side roads too. Decide where your roads are to go and plan crossing points and traffic lights at the same time. Make cardboard traffic lights, parking notices, no-waiting signs. They will stand up well if you push their bases into some model clay.

Now you can get your cars on the road. Drive them to shops, factories and offices, take the children to school and have your trucks make deliveries.

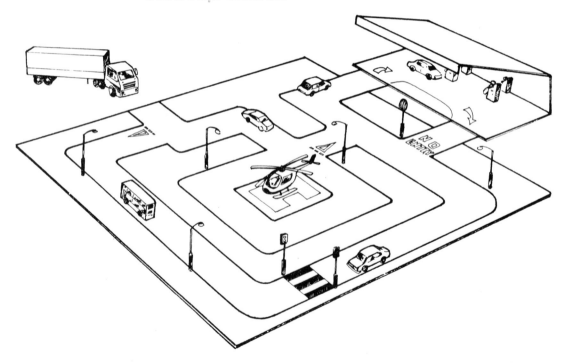

Zoo time

Here's your chance to design a zoo that all the animals would love living in. You've probably got lots of little zoo animals so divide them up into ones that can live together and ones that can't – don't put the lions in with the goats, for example. Then you can see how many different enclosures you will need.

Cut a circular shape out of foil and find some small stones or pebbles to go around the edge. This will make a good pool for the penguins or sea lions. Lay strips of cardboard down to represent the enclosure fences. If you want to make real fences, use strips of cardboard and slot them into two cardboard "feet". The feet are small squares of cardboard with a slot cut into the middle. Push these onto your cardboard fence, one at either end, and it will stand up. You can make trees and bushes in a similar way. Fences can also be made using wooden or plastic building bricks, of course.

Some zoos are so big that they have little trains running around the ground to take people from one part of the zoo to the other. So if you have a train set you could lay some track down in your zoo, too.

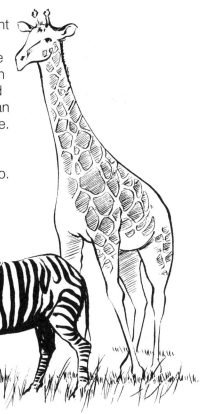

Land of the dinosaurs

Thud, crunch, creak – the dinosaurs are coming! But they need a prehistoric landscape to live in, so why not make them one?

Millions of years ago there were trees that looked very much like fir cones with spiky branches growing straight up out of the top. When you are next on a walk look out for fallen pine cones, then you can push tall, slender leaves or grasses between the 'scales'.

Another tree looked just like a long bamboo with masses of feathery foliage right at the top. To make these get a few old pea sticks, then ask someone to cut them into 30cm (12 in.) lengths.

Gather some chickweed or other plant with masses of leaves and stick the stem into the hollow middle of your bamboo. Model clay makes a good, firm base for these to stand in.

You can also draw a landscape for your monsters. Cut up a cardboard box and use just three sides of it so that it will stand up on its own as a background. With paint or felt-tipped pens, draw a rocky area with mountains and volcanoes. Collect some pebbles and stones to put in the foreground. Then make plants and trees out of thick paper or cardboard. You can use your imagination here as we do not know all the trees that were around when the dinosaurs were, so why not design your own?

Using green model clay as a base, cut out your shapes and push them into it. You can have spiky ones, feathery ones, ones like desert cacti and how about some bushes covered in exotic, tropical flowers? Your plant-eating dinosaurs would love those.

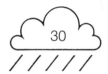
Using your marbles

Here are a couple of good ideas for using your marble collection.

For the first one you need a shoe box or some other small cardboard box. Draw three faces on one of the long sides with nice, big, wide-open mouths. The middle face should have its mouth halfway up the box. (This is to make the game a little more difficult.) You must then make a ramp so that you can roll your marbles up it and straight into the mouth. This can be made from stiff paper, as shown in the diagram.

Then decide how many points are to be awarded for each hole. Take ten marbles and roll or flick them, one at a time, into the holes from a distance of about 1.2m (4 ft). You can play this game by yourself, aiming each time to better your previous score, or you can play against a friend.

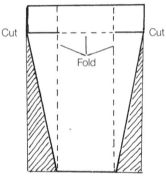

Cut · Cut · Fold

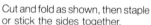

Cut and fold as shown, then staple or stick the sides together.

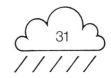
Now for the crazy marble course. Gather together some cardboard tubes, empty packets, strips of cardboard, sticky tape, scissors and a large piece of cardboard – this could be from one side of a big cardboard box.

Plan out your route, using the diagram below as a guide, and cut holes in the base board for your marbles to fall into. Then make some obstacles like the ones in the picture. You can easily make the bridge by cutting two arch shapes from stiff paper. Join them with three narrow pieces of paper, folded over at the ends and glued or stapled between the two arches. Then stick a strip of paper over these three supports so that the marbles can be sent over and under the bridge.

Give each hole a score related to its difficulty.

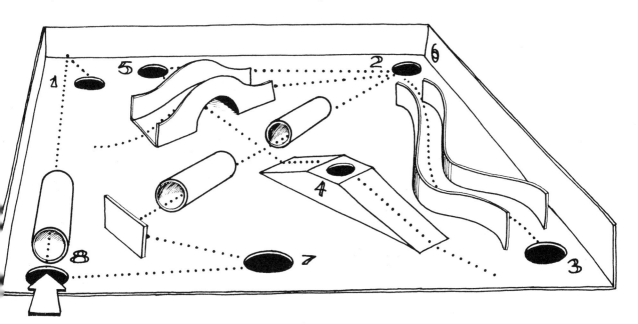

Grand prix

If you're a fan of grand prix racing then you probably have some scale models of the actual racing cars. Why not construct a circuit for them to drive on? It could be purely imaginary or might be based on a real one like Monaco, San Marino, Silverstone or Indianapolis.

Mark out the circuit by using paper strips for the sides of the track. You can cut one or two really sharp bends or winding chicanes. Don't forget to put the pits in so that the drivers can come in for a wheel change or engine check. Some tracks have bridges over them and these can be made by bending a strip of cardboard and then sticking it to a straight base which will sit on the actual track.

For the winner, make a presentation cup out of model clay. A few bricks will form the presentation rostrum from where he can shower the crowd with champagne.

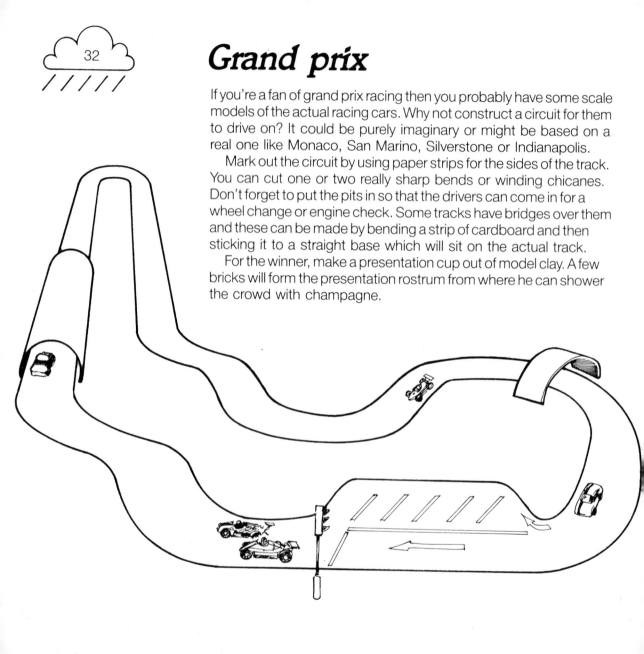

Horse trials

When it's cold, wet and·rainy outside it will cheer you up to think of summery things like horse trials or gymkhanas. Sort out the horses and ponies from your farm animals and make some fences for them to jump over.

Plastic building bricks are ideal for this as you can make fences of different heights and shapes. Make other fences using lolly sticks stuck together to form a five-bar gate. It will stand up if you stick the bottom in lumps of model clay. Cardboard tubes and matchboxes also make good fences. Decorate the sides with "shrubs", small. twigs, grass and moss stuck into a clay base.

Your horses will, of course, need stables, so see if you can find an old shoe box. The top could be used as another fence as you will need only the base. Mark out three or four stable doors, depending on the size of the box. Cut along one side and the top of each door so that they will fold back to let the horse out. Then cut into the door, halfway up, so that the horse can look out when it is locked in for the night.

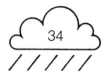

Down on the farm

Farms are often a jumble of buildings put up at different times in a higgledy-piggledy fashion. So this is a good way of using up a collection of shoe boxes and odd pieces of cardboard.

The farmhouse itself can be made out of a cardboard box. Tape up the two top flaps to form a peak. Then cut the side flaps to make central triangular shapes. Stick these to the main flaps and your pitched roof will stay in position. Now draw on doors and windows.

A shoe box will be just the thing to make a cowshed. Cut large double doors in both ends so that the cows can go in at one end to be milked and then leave by the other. Draw bricks or wooden planks on the outside to make it look more realistic.

A dutch barn will be needed to store the hay. This is a building that has a roof but is open on all four sides so that the air can circulate freely around the hay. Bend a strip of cardboard to make the roof. Then cut two semi-circular ends and fix these on with sticky tape. Attach knitting needles or straight sticks to the four corners of the roof and you have made a dutch barn.

4 Cooking is fun!

Here are seven pages of easy recipes that you can try. You may need some help with cutting up the salad ingredients or in taking the dishes out of the oven, but most of it you will be able to tackle on your own. Chilly, rainy days are good times to go into the kitchen and cook something for all the family to enjoy. It's such a warm and cosy place, and with the radio or a tape playing it's a very good way to spend an afternoon – and have something appetizing to eat at the end of it.

Before you start on any recipe, make sure you have gathered together all the ingredients and utensils that you will need. There's nothing more annoying than being covered in flour and finding that a vital ingredient is tucked away behind lots of packages. Also, if you are cooking anything in the oven, make sure you preheat it first to the temperature stated in the recipe. If you turn the oven on about ten to fifteen minutes before you put your dish in, it should be hot enough when you need it.

Dainty delights

Orange creams

This first recipe, for orange creams, can be adapted to make coffee creams and peppermint creams as well. You need the following ingredients:

200g/8oz icing sugar
  (confectioner's sugar)
1 small orange
25g/1oz butter

extra sifted icing sugar
  (confectioner's sugar)
orange jelly segments

Sift the icing sugar into a bowl, melt the butter and add this to the sugar. Grate the orange and tip this into your bowl. Cut the orange in half and squeeze out the juice. Add 2 tablespoons of the juice to the bowl and mix well. Turn your mixture out onto a board dusted with icing sugar. Knead the mixture until it is smooth and then divide it into 20 equal pieces. Roll each piece gently into a ball and then flatten it slightly. You can decorate the top with orange jelly segments, then leave in a cool place until your orange creams are firm. If you are making them for a party, why not buy some paper cases and serve them in those?

Coffee creams

Use 2 level tablespoons of instant coffee powder and 1 tablespoon of lukewarm milk instead of the orange peel and juice. Decorate with an almond or walnut.

Peppermint creams

Omit the orange peel and juice and add 1 teaspoon of peppermint essence to the sugar and melted butter. Decorate with chocolate drops.

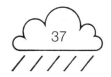

Uncooked chocolate fudge

50g/2oz plain chocolate
25g/1oz butter
1½ tablespoons fresh cream

1 teaspoon vanilla essence
200g/8oz sifted icing sugar
(confectioner's sugar)

Break up the chocolate into a basin and add the butter. Stand the basin in a saucepan of hot water. Leave until melted, stirring once or twice. Remove the basin and stir in the cream and vanilla. Gradually add the sugar and mix well. Pour into a 15cm (6in) square dish and leave in a cool place until set. Then cut into squares.

Cornflake crisp cakes

100g/4oz cooking chocolate   150g/6oz cornflakes

Melt the chocolate in a basin over a saucepan of hot, but not boiling, water. When all the chocolate has melted, stir in the cornflakes so that they are well coated with the chocolate. Then fill cake cases with the mixture and leave to set.

Fruit and nut fun balls

75g/3oz dates, stoned
50g/2oz walnuts
25g/1oz mixed peel, if liked (or add
   an extra 25g/1oz raisins)

50g/2oz raisins
2 teaspoons thick honey
shredded coconut

Chop the dates and the walnuts on a wooden board. In a basin, mix together the chopped dates and walnuts, the peel, raisins and honey. Stir the mixture with a wooden spoon until the fruit and nuts are well coated with honey. Divide the mixture into 14 pieces and shape each piece into a ball. Put some shredded coconut on a plate and roll each ball in it until it is well covered. Place the balls on a plate and eat when required.

Scrumptious salads

Apple and walnut salad

Mix the following ingredients together in a bowl:

2 sticks chopped celery
1 chopped apple
75g/3oz chopped cabbage

50g/2oz walnuts
50g/2oz raisins
1 tablespoon salad cream

Wash some leaves from an iceberg lettuce and arrange them on two plates. Divide the mixture evenly between the two plates and top the salads off with a generous tablespoon of cottage or low-fat cream cheese. Sprinkle a few more raisins on top.

Fruit salad with cheese

small can pineapple
1 sweet apple
1 banana
2 grated carrots

75g/3oz grated cheddar cheese
50g/2oz cashew nuts
50g/2oz raisins

Wash some crunchy lettuce leaves and arrange on two plates. Open a can of pineapple – tip the juice into a glass (you can drink this later with your salad).

Put the pineapple in a large mixing bowl, chop up the apple and banana and mix this in with the pineapple. Pile this mixture onto the lettuce leaves. Arrange the grated carrot around the edge of the plates. Sprinkle the cheese over and add the cashew nuts and raisins.

Eat this salad straight away or the fruit will begin to turn brown. If liked, trickle a tablespoonful of salad cream over and around your salad.

Simple pizzas

These pizzas all use bread as a base so there is no dough to make.

small can tomatoes   pepper, salt, garlic powder, mixed herbs
25g/1oz grated cheese

Cut up 1 large tomato or two small ones and add to them a pinch of salt, pepper, garlic and mixed herbs.

Toast a thick slice of bread on one side only. Spread the non-toasted side with butter or margarine, then add the tomato mixture. Sprinkle the grated cheese over and put under the grill until the cheese melts and begins to turn brown.

Eat with a green salad of lettuce, cucumber, green pepper and onions, if liked.

Ham, garlic sausage or salami pizza
You can make your pizza even tastier by adding a slice of ham, garlic sausage or salami underneath the layer of cheese.

Mushroom and green pepper pizza
Non-meat eaters can add thin slices of mushroom and green pepper underneath the cheese layer to give their pizza a different taste.

Cinnamon toast
A quickie snack is made by mixing together a knob of butter or other spread with a generous pinch of cinnamon and a ½ teaspoon of sugar.

Toast a slice of bread on both sides and spread with the cinnamon mixture. Bet you can't eat just one slice!

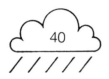

Oaty things

There are lots of exciting things to be made with rolled oats so we'll see how many recipes can be squeezed onto these two pages.

Flapjacks

100g/4oz butter or soya margarine	75g/3oz brown sugar
75g/3oz golden syrup	200g/8oz rolled oats

Turn the oven on to 180°C/350°F/gas no 4 before you begin your preparation.

Put the butter, syrup and sugar in a pan over a low heat until it has melted. Then mix in the oats and stir well. Spread the mixture over a flat, greased baking dish 20cm x 30cm (8in x 12in) and press down with a knife until smooth. As the oven will now be very hot, put the dish in carefully or ask someone older to do it for you.

Cook for 20 minutes or until the top has turned a light brown. Take out of the oven and leave for 5 minutes before cutting the flapjack into 24 pieces. Do not remove from the dish until it is quite cold. Store in an airtight container.

Oatmeal refrigerator cookies

100g/4oz butter/margarine	½ teaspoon vanilla essence
100g/4oz sugar	75g/3oz flour
100g/4oz brown sugar	½ teaspoon salt
1 egg	125g/5oz rolled oats

Preheat oven to 180°C/350°F/gas no 4.

Cream together the butter, sugars and egg. Sift together the flour and salt and add it to the butter mixture, together with the oats and vanilla essence. Blend well. Form into long rolls and refrigerate for 1 hour. Then cut into 8mm (¼in) slices.

Place on a greased baking dish 2.5cm (1in) apart and put in oven for 8-10 minutes. Makes about 24 cookies.

Home-made muesli

Serves 4

75g/3oz rolled oats
25g/1oz raisins
25g/1oz chopped dates
2 chopped dried apricots
25g/1oz shredded coconut

25g/1oz brown sugar
25g/1oz chopped nuts
25g/1oz hazelnuts
1 small banana

Mix all the ingredients together. Divide between 4 bowls, pour milk over and leave in refrigerator for 5 minutes before eating to allow milk to soak in.

Quick oatmeal crumble

50g/2oz flour
50g/2oz oatmeal
100g/4oz butter or margarine

50g/2oz sugar
can peaches

Cream together butter, sugar and oatmeal. Add the flour.
Open the can of peaches and pour into an oven-proof dish. Sprinkle the oatmeal mixture on top and bake in a preheated oven (180°C/350°C/gas no 4) for 45 minutes or until the top turns brown.
Eat with cream or yogurt.

Pastry things

You will often hear people say they can't make pastry, but it's so simple you can't go wrong.

Shortcrust pastry

200g/8oz flour	100g/4oz butter or margarine
¼ level teaspoon salt	10-12 teaspoons of cold water

Sift flour and salt into a bowl. Cut up butter or margarine into small pieces and add this to the flour, mixing in well with a fork. Then rub the mixture with *clean* fingertips until it looks like fine breadcrumbs. Add the water and blend together with the fork. When all the water is well mixed in, draw the pastry together with your fingers and knead it lightly on a floured board until it looks smooth.

Roll out on a floured pastry board.

Jam tarts

Grease some tartlet pans. Roll out the pastry and cut out some circles with a pastry cutter. Put these in the tartlet pans and add 1 teaspoonful of jam to each. Pop into a preheated oven (180°C/350°F/gas no 4) for 12 minutes.

Cheese straws

Grate 75g/3oz cheese

Roll out your pastry and sprinkle the cheese all over the middle. Fold the pastry in from all sides to cover the cheese and then roll out again. Cut the pastry into 10cm/4in lengths and lay on a greased baking dish, giving each straw a twist in the middle as you do so. Brush each straw lightly with milk and pop in a preheated oven (180°C/350°F/gas no 4) for 10-15 minutes or until they have turned a golden brown.

5 Party games

There's no better way of breaking the ice at a party than by playing a few silly games. But parties don't happen that often, so why not invite a few friends over and brighten up a dull day? Ask the family to join in, too.

Some of the games in this chapter need to be made or prepared a little in advance so plan ahead and you will have a really good time. It could turn into an impromptu party. Ask each of your friends to bring some food with them and have an indoor picnic after you've worked your way through all these games.

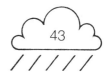

In the rush hour

If you've ever been caught up in the morning or evening rush hour you'll know how difficult it is to read a newspaper.

In this game you all have to imagine you're sitting in a crowded train or bus. Arrange two lines of chairs so that they face one another and there are no gaps in between. Also place a chair at either end, facing into the middle.

Before your party starts, mix up a number of newspapers so that their pages are in the wrong order and some are upside down. Give each player one of the mixed-up newspapers. Someone blows a whistle or shouts "go" then everyone must try to put their paper back into its correct order.

It won't be as easy as it sounds, but the first one to do so is the winner.

Pin the tail on the donkey

Trying to pin the tail on the donkey, while blindfolded, is difficult and funny, but attempting to pin on an ear and an eye as well is hilarious and almost impossible.

Draw the outline of a donkey on a large sheet of paper and stick it on the door or wall with sticky pads or pins. Then draw and cut out a tail, an ear and a nice big eye. Put a sticky pad on each of these and blindfold the first contestant. Now hand over the tail, ear and eye that will complete the donkey and see how close this contestant comes to getting it right.

You could divide the donkey up into points so that "very close" wins 10 points, "a near miss" gains 5 and "miles away" gets 0.

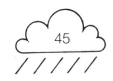
Treasure trail

Only the answers to the treasure trail clues will lead you to the treasure! If you want to play the game, too, ask an adult to write some clues for you and hide the treasure before the party begins. There will be two teams and two routes to the treasure so you will need two different sets of clues. The clues shouldn't be too easy nor so hard that it takes ages to solve each one of them.

Each team follows its own clues and route and the team who finds the treasure first keeps it. Chocolate money would make an ideal hoard. Perhaps there should be a consolation prize for the losers, too.

Stampede

Put all the chairs in a circle or tell everyone to sit on cushions in a ring on the floor. If there are eleven people playing, two will be lions, two tigers, two elephants, two giraffes and two gorillas and one will sit in the middle. If you have an even number of people playing, then you will have to have three of one kind of animal.

The person sitting in the middle calls out the name of one of the animals — perhaps "elephant" — and the two elephants change places while the person in the middle tries to get to one of the places first. If he or she is successful then the "animal" without a seat or cushion goes in the middle and the other person becomes the elephant.

Every so often "stampede" may be called. Then everyone has to get up and change seats while the person in the middle again attempts to get a seat in the ring.

Can you draw me? ✓

This sounds a very easy game, but is it? You need lots of large pieces of paper, or a board and easel would do just as well.

Before blindfolding one of your guests, ask him or her to try to draw one of the other people in the room. Give the artist a minute or two to study the subject then put the blindfold on. Hand him different pencils for each part of the face – black for the outline, blue for the eyes, red for the mouth, brown for the hair and so on. There's little chance that this portrait will be very life-like!

Querky quoits

You really need a sheet of plywood for this game unless you have some very thick cardboard.

Draw a clown or juggler onto your board and give him some bright clothes. Then screw little hooks into the board, positioning them near his hat, chest, hands and feet so that when the quoits are thrown onto the board it looks as though your clown is juggling.

The quoits themselves can be made from florists' wire, twisted into a circle and covered with crepe paper, or you could use the circular top from a margarine tub, carefully cutting out the middle. Give each hook a number so that you can total up your score at the end. You can make as many quoits as you like, but you will need at least three.

Relay race

Divide into two teams. Each 'leg' of the race is one length of the room and there are four 'legs' in all: fanning butterflies, hopping frogs, pushing marbles and blowing a ping-pong ball. The "butterflies" are paper handkerchiefs, tied in the middle with a piece of cotton or sticky tape. You fan them with a sheet of paper to get them to move along the carpet. If you have some tiddly winks, use these for your hopping frogs, otherwise use buttons. Pushing marbles along sounds easy – except you must do it with your nose. And blowing a ping-pong ball is just what it says it is!

   If you have more than four people in each team, just repeat the relays until everyone has had a go. The first team to finish is, of course, the winner.

Musical statues

In musical statues you must move or dance to the music and when it stops you freeze and stay in that position until the music starts again. You have to remain still for 30 seconds, but during that time, the judge will walk among you to make sure you aren't moving. He can try and make you laugh, but mustn't touch you.

   Anyone who moves is out. If no one has moved after 30 seconds then the music plays and they all come to life again. The winner is the only one remaining at the end.

What is it?

The object of this game is to guess what's inside the box. You are allowed to feel it, but not, of course, to see it. Easy enough, you think? Well, not if you're wearing a nice pair of thick woolly gloves!

Two holes must be cut in the side of a cardboard box, just large enough for your hands to get through. Make sure the top of the box is secured so that it doesn't pop open at the wrong moment.

Collect together a lot of different objects and place them in the box, three at a time. Give each contestant a pen and paper. Then the first one puts the gloves on and tries to guess what the objects are. Set a time limit of one minute and at the end of that time, the gloves and box are passed to the next person while the first contestant writes the answers down. The box could be filled three or four times, then, at the end of all the rounds, the person with the most correct answers wins.

What a smell! /

How good is your sense of smell? This game is a quiet one to play after something hectic like musical chairs or stampede. Before your party begins, find six or eight clean yogurt or cream pots and put a smelly substance in each. Then cover the tops with foil and secure with an elastic band. Make tiny holes in the top of the foil so that the smell can waft out, but no one can see what is inside.

Then ask each competitor in turn to smell the pot and write down the answer. The one with most correct answers wins.

Some nice smelly things you could put in your pots are curry powder, garlic, vinegar, peppermint essence, lemon, orange, rose petals, cucumber, mustard, cloves, tea, coffee.

Tiddlywink obstacle course

If you haven't any counters then buttons can be used in this game. You can play it either on your own or with friends. Scoring works in the same way as in a game of golf, so add up how many "winks" it takes to conquer each obstacle.

Make six or eight obstacles and place them around the floor. You could have an egg cup; a "fence" to jump over, made from building bricks; a flower pot; a "water jump", made by placing two pencils 20 cm (8 in) apart; a platform jump that is four books piled one on top of the other – the object is to land the counter on the top; a large circle made with a length of wool – this is a bunker that the counter must avoid; a beaker or mug; a piece of paper 2.5 cm (1 in) square on which the counter must land.

If you are playing the game alone then time yourself to see how long it takes.

Beetle

Beetle can be played with any number of players. All you need are pencils, some paper and a dice. The object of the game is to see who can complete their beetle first. The first person to throw a six starts. He or she must then throw another six for the body before the other parts can be drawn. Once you have the body, you then need a 5 or 4 for thorax or back legs, and so on up the body. If you make a successful throw you can have another go.

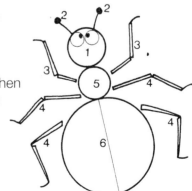

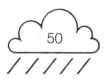

How nosey!

Two empty matchboxes are all you need to play this game. Divide your party guests into two teams – if there is an odd number then one person can be the referee to make sure there is no foul play. Make two long lines. The first player places the matchbox on his or her nose. The matchbox is then passed down the line from nose to nose without using hands, feet or anything else to help it along. If it falls to the floor, you may then use your hands to put it back on your nose. If there is a tie, the number of times the matchbox fell off will count against the score.

Chin-chin! / balloons-

This is a similar idea to the matchbox game, but here an orange is passed along the line. The first person places the orange underneath his chin and the second person attempts to take it over by placing it beneath his or her chin, again without any help from the hands. Don't squeeze the orange too hard or you will have a nasty sticky fruit to pass down the line which will be a little uncomfortable – not to say messy. Under these circumstances, the rules say you can have another orange.

To make both games harder still, blindfold each player as it comes to their turn. Don't blindfold the whole team at once or nobody will know what's happening!

A referee is essential if you are playing the games blindfold so that the players can be pointed in the right direction if they are going hopelessly astray.

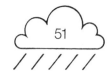

6 Card and board games

Your house probably has several packs of cards, but maybe doesn't
have so many board games. If you want to play snakes and ladders,
but haven't got a set it's very easy to make your own. The following
pages contain instructions for making and playing some board
games and card games.

Snakes and ladders

Divide a sheet of paper into 100 squares, with ten along each side. Snakes and ladders boards usually tell little stories. People slide down snakes when they've done something bad and climb up ladders when they've been good or helpful. Draw in your snakes and ladders, some short and some long – it is particularly cunning to have a snake a few squares away from the end so when someone thinks they are about to win they land on a snake and have to slither back down it again.

Then draw in some little pictures so that a good deed leads up a ladder and a bad deed sends you down again. For instance, helping around the house would send you up a ladder, throwing litter on the floor would send you down.

Each player needs a counter and the person who throws a six first starts. Everyone then takes a turn to have a throw and the first one to reach square 100 is the winner.

Shove ha'penny

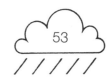

A shove ha'penny board is very easy to make. You need a piece of stiff cardboard 1m (3ft) long and 45cm (18in) wide. Draw lines all the way down the cardboard 5cm (2in) apart.

At the edge of the board write in a number for each space; you can decide which numbers go where, but you must have the highest numbers at the top of the board as they are the most difficult to attain.

The game is very simple. Just put a coin on the bottom edge of the board and hit it with the heel of your hand. You score only if the coin is sitting exactly in the space and is not partially covering a line. However, if you feel this is too difficult and making scoring almost impossible, then score half marks for any coin sitting on a line.

Each player should have six coins and the one who scores the highest wins.

You could decide that the one who reaches 100 first wins, or even set the limit at 200 if you have some real experts playing.

This can also be played as a team game so the first team to reach, say, 250 wins. This is a very good game to play at a party just after all the birthday food has been eaten. It is non-energetic so no one will feel ill!

Tiddlywink birds

Tiddlywink birds can be played with counters, if you have them, or buttons if you haven't. Find a big piece of cardboard, the larger the better; the bottom of a box picked up at the supermarket would be ideal.

In the middle of the cardboard you are going to stick five birds. You can either draw them or cut them out of a magazine. Position them so that each is approximately 7.5cm (3in) away from any other bird. Now write a value on each one from 1-5.

Draw ten wriggly worms on a sheet of paper and cut these out also. Any number of people can play this game. All you need are five small counters, or buttons, and one larger one to "wink" them with. Each player takes it in turn to "wink" his five counters onto a bird. The one with the highest score at the end of the round wins that round and is presented with a wriggly worm. At the end of ten rounds the person with the most wriggly worms is the winner.

Each counter can only be winked twice and then the score is added up, even if no points have been won. Draw a circle at one edge of the board so that all the players start from the same point.

Dominoes

Match the number

Each player takes seven dominoes. If there are less than four people playing the remaining dominoes are used as "stock" and as one person lays a domino down he then takes one from stock. The object is to get rid of all your dominoes first and try to block the way of the other players. You will see how to do this the more you play the game.

The first player lays down a domino which should be a double. If it is a double six, the next player must lay a domino with a six on it next to the first one. Suppose a 6 with a 2 is laid, the following player must lay a 2 next to the 2 or a 6 next to the first double that was laid.

If a player cannot go she must miss a turn and wait until she is able to go, but only when her turn comes around again.

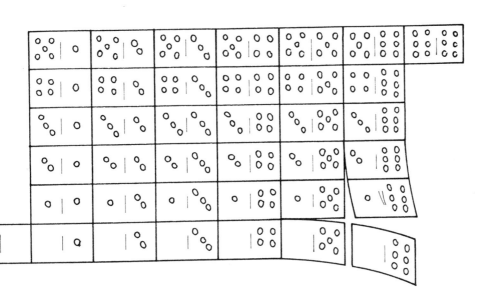

Card games

Matching pairs

This card game tests your memory and powers of observation. It is best played with two to four players, but it is possible to play it with almost any number.

The cards are shuffled and then spread out on the floor or table face down. The first player turns over two cards. If they have the same value, say, two fours or two kings, then he keeps them and has another go. If two different cards are turned up they must be turned over again in exactly the same position.

Everyone must watch this very closely to try to remember the position of those cards in case they turn over a matching one. The person with the most pairs at the end of the game wins.

Snap

This is really a game for two players, although three or four can play it. Each player is dealt an equal number of cards and places them in a stack face down. The first player lays a card in the middle of the table. The next person lays one on top and so on around the table. If the card is the same value as the one already on the table, the first person to shout "snap" wins all the cards in the middle pile. The game is over when one person has won all the cards.

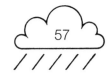

Old Maid

The object of this game is simply not to lose, for the loser is the one holding the Old Maid card at the end. This is a game for three or more players.

Take a pack of cards and remove one queen. Then deal all the cards out, starting by giving one to the player on your left and so on right round the table. Do this until all the cards have been dealt out; it does not matter if some players have more than others.

Each player fans his cards out and looks at them without letting anyone else see what is in his hand. If there are any pairs – two fours or two kings, for instance – these may be laid face down on the table. If a player has three kings he may still lay only two of them down and must wait until he has a fourth king to make another pair.

The game begins by the dealer offering his fanned out cards to the player on his left, still making sure that no one sees what cards he has in his hand. The player on the left selects one card, unseen, and places it with his other cards. If this card matches any in his hand he may lay that pair down. If not, he keeps it and offers all his cards to the player on his left who now selects one. This goes on until all the cards have been laid down in pairs and one player is left with the odd queen – the Old Maid.

My ship sails

If you look at a pack of playing cards you will see that there are four different designs: hearts, clubs, diamonds and spades. These are called "suits". The object of this game is to be the first person to collect seven cards of the same suit.

From four to seven people can play this. Each player is dealt seven cards and the remaining ones are not used. She then looks at her cards and decides which suit she will try to collect. She may change her mind as the game progresses.

Each player then discards one card that she does not want by placing it face down and pushing it to the player on her left who picks it up. Each player then selects another unwanted card (it may be the one she has just picked up) and pushes this to the left as before. The game proceeds until one player has seven cards of the same suit when she shouts out "my ship sails".

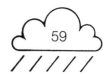
7 Entertain your friends

Ask your friends if they know any magic tricks or card tricks and then put on a show for your families. They might prefer to make some of the puppets described on pages 66 and 67 and write a little play for them. Then they could give a performance in between the other items in the show.

Go over your own act several times, so that the audience will not immediately guess how the tricks are done.

Add in some musical items played on your newly-made instruments (see pages 60 and 61) and you have all the ingredients of a varied and entertaining show.

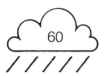

Pump up the volume

Have you often longed to have your own drum kit? Well here's a very inexpensive way of making your own then you can play drum solos whenever you feel like it.

First of all, gather together a number of cans of different sizes. Then you need some strong brown paper, sticky tape and scissors. Put one of your cans on the brown paper and draw a circle around it, 10cm (4 in.) bigger than the can. Cut out your circle and wet the paper, then pull it tightly over the open end of your can. Stick the sides down with tape, making sure you are keeping the paper as taut as possible. Finally, run a length of sticky tape right around the edge of the circle, securing it firmly to the can.

Knitting needles work quite well as drumsticks, but for a louder and deeper sound you could fix a wooden bead to the ends.

The drums will sound better if you can raise them off the floor, so find a box that will fit over a stool or small table or taller box, then tape each can to it in order of pitch.

Doh-ray-me ...

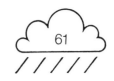

Here are two ways of making musical instruments that play a scale – doh, ray, me, fah, soh, lah, te, doh. You will need eight glass bottles and a stick to tap them with. Fill each with different levels of water in descending order and keep testing the sound by tapping each bottle with your stick until you are satisfied with the result. Now try out some simple tunes, like nursery rhymes. Sing them to yourself and try to decide which bottle produces which note. You'll soon get the hang of it.

If yours is a do-it-yourself household then you probably have lots of odds and ends of wood lying around. Ask a parent or older brother or sister to cut you eight lengths of wood, each one 2.5cm (1 in) longer than the previous one. Then tie all these evenly together with string and hang from a nail or picture hook, as shown in the picture. Then with another piece of wood or knitting needle you can tap out a tune as you did with the bottles.

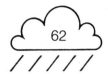
Telepathy

This really does look like magic to those who don't know how it's done. You must work with a partner, but, first of all, put your finger tips to the side of your head about level with your eyes. Now clench your jaws, can you feel a movement there? This is how this form of telepathy works.

Now amaze your friends with your telepathic powers. Ask someone to blindfold you, then ask him or her to hold up some fingers and you will tell everyone, by the process of telepathy, how many fingers are being shown. You then place your fingers on both sides of your friend's head. She then slowly clenches and unclenches her jaw the correct number of times so that you can proclaim the right answer. If your partner is careful, the audience should not be able to see her jaw move.

You can make it more complicated by saying you will add numbers or subtract, even multiply and divide, providing your partner is good at doing quick calculations!

4   8   15
  5   9   21

Black magic

Here again, as with telepathy, you need a partner who is in on the act.

Tell your audience that you will go out of the room and while you are away they must choose an object. When you come back in you will tell them what they have chosen. Your partner will name several things and you will say whether any one of them is the correct object. Your friends will be astonished when you get it right.

The secret is this: your partner will name several objects like a flower, cushion, lamp and vase. You will say "no" to all of these. Then he will name something that is black, like the cat or someone's shoes. This is the signal you have been waiting for. You now know that the next object will be the one that was selected. So when your partner says "clock" you can say, confidently, "yes".

Don't be tempted to try it more than a couple of times with the same people or they may soon realize how it is done.

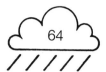

Clever paper-clips

You can be sure that all the best tricks have been rehearsed many times over before the conjurer performing them is satisfied that he can mystify his audience.

In this trick you will assure your audience that although you are putting separate paper-clips into an envelope, once inside, they will form themselves into a chain.

You need to prepare this trick well before your audience arrives. Make a chain of six paper-clips. Put this chain into a large envelope and tip it into one corner. Then run a thin line of glue insided the envelope to seal off that corner. You could also use double-sided sticky tape which would do the job just as well.

When you start your trick, ask a member of your audience to drop six separate paper-clips into the envelope, one at a time. Seal the envelope and tap it three times with your wand or say some magic words over it. Then push your sleeves up in a theatrical manner so that your audience can see that you have nothing concealed there and proceed to cut the corner off your envelope. The chain of paper clips will fall out as the audience gasps.

Make sure you cut the right corner, though, or the trick will go horribly wrong!

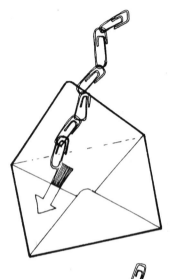

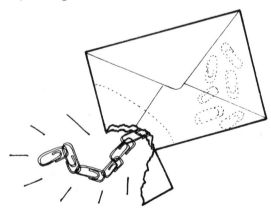

Magic matchbox

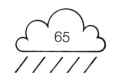

Prepare your matchbox before your guests arrive. Pass a length of thread through the tray of the matchbox from one end to the other. Then find a small piece of wood or an eraser that will just fit into the matchbox. Place this on top of the thread then put the cover back on the matchbox.

Tell your audience that although the matchbox will slide freely down the piece of thread, when you command it to stop it will do so. Hold one end of the thread in your right hand and the other in your left. Position your hands one above the other and keep the thread taut. As you loosen the thread slightly the matchbox will begin to move down. Shout "stop" as you pull the thread tight and the matchbox will stop once again.

Rehearse this trick well before you perform it so that you know by exactly how much you can loosen the thread to allow the matchbox to move freely.

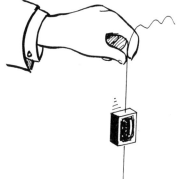

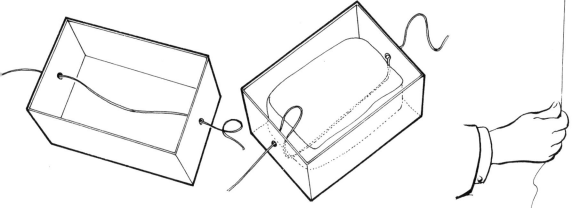

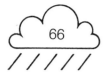
Playing with puppets

There are five different kinds of puppets on these two pages and they take just a few minutes to make but will give you hours of fun.

Elephant puppet

This glove puppet is designed so that the trunk can be worked by your longest finger. Your elephant will accept food, drink water (or pretend to) or just wave his trunk about. To make it you must cut out two elephant shapes from pieces of felt, as here. They must be large enough to fit onto your hand and the trunk should be just a little wider than your finger. Remember also to allow room for the seam. Now sew the two pieces together, all around the head and trunk, leaving just the opening for your hand. Stitch on two ears, two eyes and two tusks and your elephant is complete.

Goldilocks glove puppet

This is the more usual type of glove puppet, made in a similar way to the elephant. Two pieces of material are cut out to resemble the puppet in the picture, which looks a little like Goldilocks. Sew the two together as before, then add in the details: a frill and buttons on the dress, yellow wool for the hair and the face can be drawn in with felt-tipped pens. This puppet is worked with the thumb in one arm, the next two fingers in the head and the next finger in the arm. The little finger isn't needed.

Sock puppets

The dog and dragon are both made from old socks. Put one on your hand dividing your fingers so that the thumb forms the lower jaw and the four fingers make the shape of the top of the head. When you are wearing the sock on your hand you will see where the detail has to go. With a felt-tipped pen, mark the position of the nose, eyes, ears, tongue and any other details like the scales that stick up on

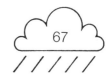

the dragon. Take the sock off and sew on the eyes, ears etc. When you put the sock back on again, your creature will come to life.

Finger puppets

The finger puppets shown here are made out of paper but you could also use felt for a longer-lasting toy.

The paper ones are quite simple to make. Roll a piece of paper around your finger so that it fits quite well without falling off every time you move it. Stick the paper together and make another tube in the same way. Then draw on the face and any other details. Here the knight has a sword, helmet and shield. His lady is going to watch while he fights the dragon – then it's her turn!

Yet more finger puppets

To make this footballer finger puppet you will need some fairly stiff cardboard. Draw the top half of the body only as your fingers will be the "legs". Cut out two circles at hip height, large enough to fit over the index finger and middle finger. Push the footballer onto your fingers and just watch him run!

Puppet show

Now you've made some puppets you will need a building for them to perform in. There's quite a lot of cutting to do here so it might be wise to get some help. Find a cardboard box at least 60cm (2ft) long and 30cm (12in) deep and cut off all the top flaps. Stick two of these on the side of the front of the box to conceal some of the action that is going on backstage. Cut out a large rectangle from the front of the box leaving a 5cm (2in) border remaining to keep it stable.

Before you start to add the scenery or other decoration you must cut a hole in the bottom of your box 10cm (4in) wide by 30cm (12in) deep. It should be no more than 5cm (2in) away from the back of the box. When you set up your puppet show on the table this part will overhang so that you can get your hands up onto the stage to manipulate the puppets.

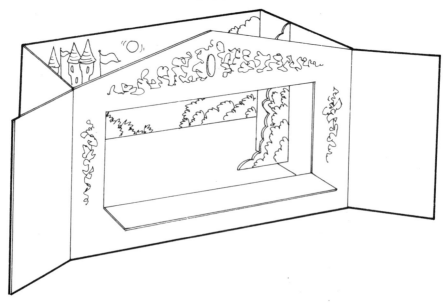

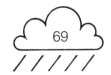
8 The appliance of science

This chapter's called The Appliance of Science because everything in it, however simple, has a scientific base, perhaps depending on sound waves, gravity, or the laws of motion to make it work. You may already have come across some of them in science lessons in school, but we hope some will be new to you. No special equipment is needed, most things will be found in your kitchen or elsewhere in the house. Some of them you can even use to entertain friends when your birthday comes around.

Turning white flowers blue

You may ask, "What's the point of turning white flowers blue or red or yellow when you can easily go into a shop and buy some?" The answer is that it's fun! and quite fascinating to watch it happening. It would definitely cheer up a younger brother or sister who is unwell or bored.

   Add ink or blue food dye to half a jar of water. Stand a white flower in the jar and wait for dramatic things to happen. You could, of course, use red, yellow, green or orange – in fact, a green flower would look very strange. If the flower has not been freshly picked, trim off the bottom of the stem which will have dried up and the experiment will not work as well, if at all.

   After about an hour you will see the flower begin to change, starting with the tips of the petals. If you stand it in clear water again, the blue will begin to fade and the flower will become white again. Try also standing a yellow flower in blue water. The tips of the petals will turn green and you will have a very attractive and unusual flower.

Water magnifying glass

Did you know that water is a natural magnifying agent? Try this experiment and you will see for yourself.

Bend a piece of thin wire to form a loop at one end about 1cm (½in) across. Dip the loop into a bowl of water and a drop should stay within the loop. Have something ready that you wish to magnify – a leaf, some small print or a tiny insect. Your drop of water will magnify your subject between four and five times its actual size.

Bush telephone

To make a bush telephone you need a piece of string approximately 20 metres (65ft) long and two empty cans. Make sure the edges are completely smooth. Make a hole in the bottom of each can with a nail and then thread the ends of the string through these holes and knot them on the insides.

Ask a friend to take one can and then walk away from you until the string is straight and taut. By speaking into the cans you will be able to have a conversation in a normal speaking voice.

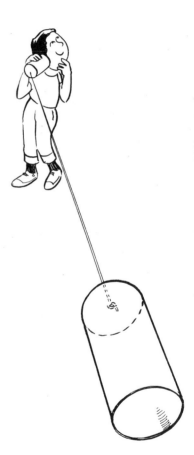

Whizz bang

This toy may well give you lots of fun, but may not be very popular with those around you! It's only made from cardboard and brown paper but it produces a satisfyingly big BANG.

Cut out a triangle from some thin cardboard – an old cereal packet would do – so that one side (ABC) is 30cm (12in) long. Cut a smaller triangle out of brown paper, but this time there must be two sides of equal length (XY and YZ) 15cm (6in) long. Join side XY to AB and YZ to BC with sticky tape and fold the two triangles in half as shown. Now tuck the brown paper flap inside the cardboard triangle and fold it flat.

Hold your whizz bang up in the air by the pointed end and bring it down sharply. You will hear a nice big bang that will make everyone jump.

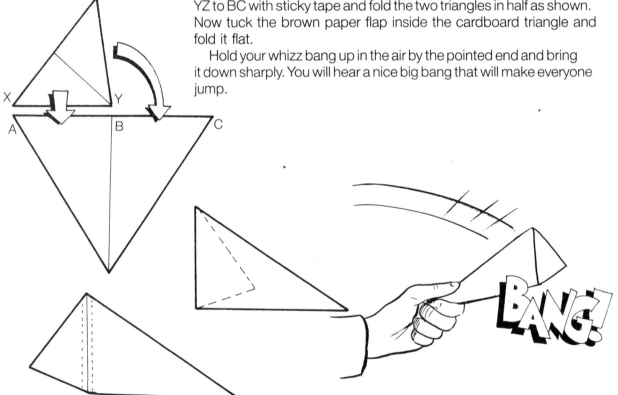

Magic fountain

This is a quick way of making your own indoor fountain. You need a bottle with a screw top, a drinking straw, a nail to fit in the end, some model clay and a bowl.

Make a hole in the middle of the screw top and push the straw through. Plug all the gaps around the straw with the model clay. Half fill the bottle with water and add a little blue ink. Screw the top on and stand the bottle in the bowl. Put the nail in the end of the straw to make it airtight. Then pour hot tap water into the bowl, remove the nail and wait for your fountain to work. As soon as the air inside the bottle begins to warm up, water will be forced up through the straw and the fountain will begin to spurt out.

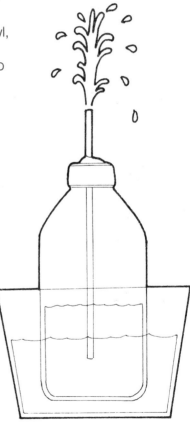

Messing about in boats

Matchbox boats

Matchbox boats are very quick and easy to make. For a very simple model you need one matchbox, a small stick and a small rectangle of paper.

If you have two matchboxes, push the two trays halfway into either end of one of the covers. Use a stick for the mast. For the sail, cut out a triangular piece of paper or material and stick two matchsticks to the top of the sail. Tie cotton to all three corners then attach the sail to the boats as shown.

Paddleboats

The paddleboat is made out of thick cardboard. Cut out the main piece as shown and put a notch on the outer edge of each "leg". Then cut two rectangular pieces for the paddles. Make a slot halfway along each of these strips then push the two pieces together. Fix them to the paddleboat with an elastic band, making sure it rests in the two notches. Wind the rubber band around several times, then lower your paddleboat gently into the water. Just watch it go!

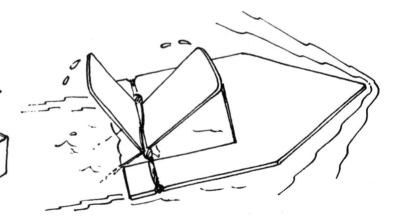

Launch the shuttle

A super high-flying space shuttle can be made from some very basic
materials. All you need are two used matchsticks (choose the
thickest ones), some stiff paper, a small piece of model clay and a
strong elastic band. First, make the plane. Cut out the shuttle wing
shape from your stiff paper and glue your matchstick to its middle.
Then cut out a small tail fin and stick this on, too. Put a small lump
of model clay on the nose end of the shuttle to help its balance.

The launch pad is made by pushing a match through the
matchbox and stretching the elastic band around the matchbox as
shown. Now lay the shuttle inside the elastic band, pull the
matchstick down and your shuttle will make an amazingly good
take-off.

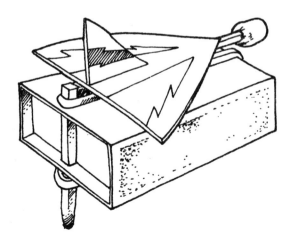

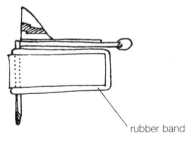

rubber band

Grow your own crystals

This experiment looks quite magical – crystals appear as if from nowhere. Everything you need should be around the house, but you may have to buy some washing soda as it isn't used as much as it once was.

Fill a jam jar with very hot water and begin to dissolve teaspoonsful of washing soda in it. Stir well to make sure it dissolves quickly and keep adding the washing soda until the mixture becomes so saturated that it no longer dissolves it.

At this point, tie a button to a stick, pen or pencil that will rest on the rim of the jar. The thread should be just long enough for the button to be suspended in about half the depth of water. Put the jar in a safe place where it cannot easily be knocked over by dogs, cats or small children and then wait for your crystals to grow. It shouldn't be too long before you see the first ones appear on the button.

Stalagmites and stalactites

You've no doubt seen pictures of underground caves with long thin stalagmites and stalactites growing from floor and ceiling – perhaps you've even visited some yourself. You can make your own miniature ones by using washing soda dissolved in water, as on the previous page. Then you can see how the real ones are formed. They, of course, take hundreds and thousands of years to grow, whereas you will only have to wait a few hours.

This time you must dissolve the washing soda in two jars of hot water. As before, keep adding the soda until the solution will not dissolve any more. Then stand the jars a little way apart from each other with a saucer in between. Cut a length of wool, twist it into a rope and stand one end in each jar with the middle hanging down over the saucer. The soda solution will soak up and along the wool until it begins to drip on the plate forming little stalagmites and stalactites.

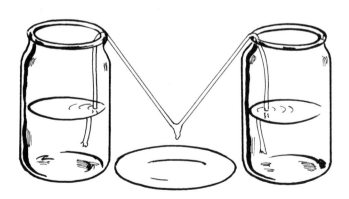

Indoor lightning

You can see the results of this better if the room is totally dark, so this is definitely an experiment to be carried out in the evening. You need a large metal tray, a ball of soft model clay, a polythene bag and a metal lid or badge.

Stand the tray on the polythene bag and stick the clay in the middle of the tray. Conduct your experiment near a light switch or table lamp so that someone can switch the lights out at just the right moment. Now, holding only the clay, push the tray around and around over the polythene bag as quickly as you can. Do this for several minutes and have the lid ready. Now turn out the lights and swiftly bring the lid nearer the rim of the tray without actually touching it. You will see a flash of static electricity move between the tray and the metal lid.

If the results are not very good the first time, it may mean that you didn't rub the tray on the polythene bag long and hard enough. Try again.

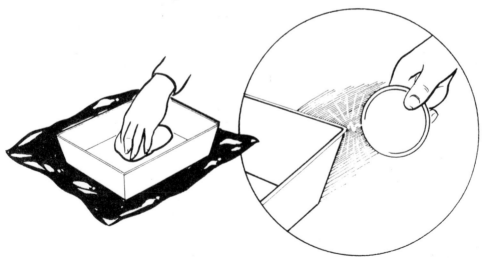

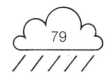

9 Before your very eyes

This chapter is all about optical toys – that is, toys that rely on what the eye sees, or thinks it sees, for their effect. As you will realize when you read through the chapter, toys like these fascinated our great-great-grandparents. Both children and adults thought they were great fun and as each new optical toy was produced every household wanted to own one.

Visit your local museum some time to see if they have any other optical toys that are not included here. They should also have examples of peepshows, tops, zoetropes, flicker books and "turning wonders". They might like to see the ones you have made, too.

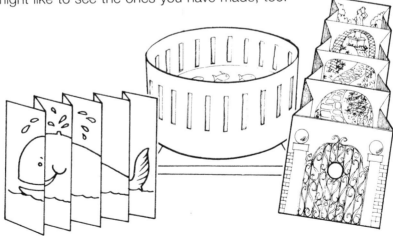

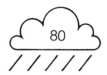
Peep shows

Peep shows were very popular in Victorian times when children had few toys. They were often made to commemorate an important national event, a great exhibition or the opening of some imposing building when they would become a feature in the parlour and a conversation piece for the adults. They are rarely seen now except in museums although they are occasionally made, usually with an historical theme, and it is most likely that they would be sold by museums.

You can, of course, make your own. There are two kinds. One that closes concertinawise and the other that is made in a shoe box. You will see from the illustration that, in order to make the kind that concertinas, you need one very long piece of paper or several smaller ones joined together. Glue the ends together so that it makes a long thin box shape. Then choose your subject. If you are going to make a garden like the one in the illustration you must first make a plan of how you are going to design it. Make "dividers" so that your box will be divided into six separate equal parts. These should have arches cut in them with a trellis surrounding each one. Make these dividers slightly wider than the box, then fold down a narrow margin on both sides and glue these to the sides of the box. Cut a small hole in the front of the box just large enough to enable you to peer through. When the peep show is complete you must fold it up concertinawise. Store it flat and then all you have to do is unfold it again when you show it to your friends.

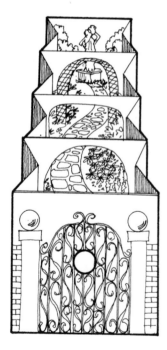

Peep show in a shoe box

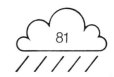

The shoe box peep show is made in a very similar way. It does not, of course, fold up and because there is a lid you will need to cut out two small rectangles to let the light in or you won't be able to see anything at all! Cut one rectangle in the lid, fairly near to the front and cut another in one side, just beyond halfway. Don't forget to cut a viewing hole, as well.

A soft light is best and this will be achieved by covering the holes with tissue paper. It can be white, but green or blue will give an eerie light while orange or yellow will give a brighter, sunnier one.

The view here is of a spaceship control room with a large window at the end looking out into deepest space. If you cover the top and side holes with blue tissue paper this should give it just the atmosphere and lighting that it needs.

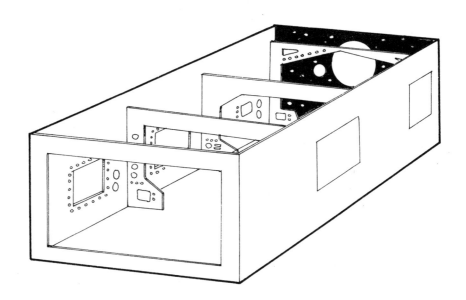

Tops and ...

These create optical illusions because you draw one design on them, but when they are spun or whizzed around another pattern appears.

Cut out a number of circles approximately 7.5cm (3in) across from thin, white cardboard. Draw on your design. Experiment with various black and white geometric patterns and use orange with red, yellow with blue, and red with blue for some interesting effects. Try out other combinations as well. If you use mauve, blue, green, yellow, orange and red in segments radiating out from the middle you should get a surprising result.

To make a spinning top you need one of these decorated circles and a short length cut from a thin dowel rod. A piece about 10cm (4in) long will be big enough. Use a pencil sharpener to fine down one end to a point. Make a hole right in the middle of the circle, and, with the patterned side uppermost, push the pointed end of the dowel through so that there is just 3cm (1¾in) showing on the underside of the circle. You can use the same piece of dowel for several different circles unless, of course, you want to set two or three spinning at the same time.

...whizzers

String-operated whizzers are equally easy to construct. First of all, cut out a circle and draw a pattern on both sides. Then, using a darning needle or hole punch, make two holes about 1.5cm (¾in) apart, both being an equal distance from the middle. Cut 1m (40in) of thin string and thread this through the two holes and knot the ends together.

Hold the two ends of the string and pull it straight. Then wind the string up by spinning the whizzer over and over until the string is well twisted. Then give it a sharp tug and pull it straight. The whizzer will unwind and the patterns on the revolving circle will appear to change.

You can add noise as well by punching holes around the edge or by cutting a serrated edge. It will then make a whooshing sound when spun which gives your whizzer even more entertainment value!

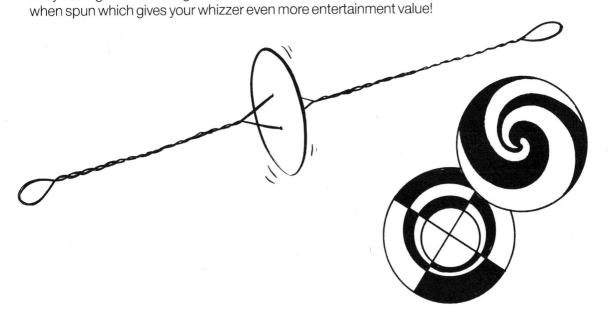

Now you see it ...

To turn winter into summer you need a sheet of typing paper or notepaper that isn't too thick. On one side, draw a wintry scene in black felt-tipped pen. Include some bare trees and perhaps a hillside. Then attach your drawing to the window, plain side facing you. The design will show through and you should draw over all the lines in pencil. This will be your summer scene. Put leaves on the trees, grass in the fields and on the hillside and clumps of flowers everywhere. Make the sky a pale blue with a bright yellow sun.

Now show your friends the winter scene and tell them you can change it to summer in a second. After the choruses of "Oh, no you can't" have died down, gradually hold your picture up to a light so that the summer side shows through.

Then you can all think of other scenes you can change in this way.

... now you don't

You *can* draw the pictures for this changing scene or you can cut them from a magazine. Choose two opposing subjects. Here we are changing a mouse into an elephant. You could change a fish into a whale or make an acorn grow into an oak. The method is quite simple. Take the back of an old birthday card and paste your two pictures either side of it. Now cut the card into five equal strips.

With clear sticky tape, hinge these strips onto a piece of card so that when laid flat you see the complete picture again. Now attach two supports to the outer edges of the strips, again using clear sticky tape. You will find that if you push your supports up you have one picture, but if you pull them down you can see the other. This would make an excellent birthday card for someone special.

Zoetrope

The idea behind this zoetrope (pronounced zo-ee-trope) is very simple. You look through slots on the outside of a revolving drum onto a series of pictures inside. Because the drum is revolving, the pictures appear to move.

To make one, you require various bits of equipment. First of all, you need a round metal container for the drum. The next thing to find is a thick square of wood to provide a firm stand for your zoetrope. Now you will have to ask for some help because a hole has to be drilled in the bottom of the drum and a bolt fixed in to the middle of the piece of wood. The drum is fitted over the bolt with two or three washers in between to allow it to revolve freely.

Then measure around the drum and cut a strip of black paper to this length, but the height should be twice that of the drum. This will be stuck inside the drum, but before you do so, cut twelve slots in the upper half of the paper – each one 8mm (¼in) wide and an equal distance away from the next one.

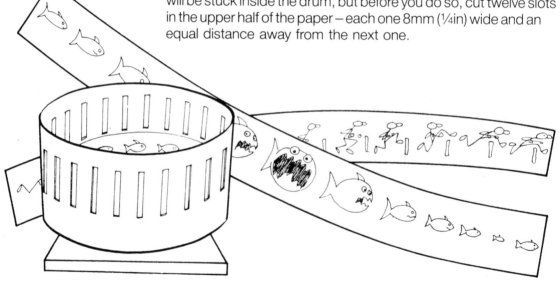

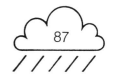

The final stage is to draw twelve little pictures in sequence. It could be hurdlers or fish, as here, but draw them so that when the strip of paper is inside the lower half of the drum, the first and last pictures form part of a never-ending sequence. Make a slot in one edge of the paper and a tab at the other so that it can be fixed securely inside the drum and can be stored flat when not in use. You can make lots more picture strips and maybe get your friends to think up some subjects as well.

Now spin the drum and peer through one of the slots. Two other people can also watch the "show" at the same time.

Flicker books

This is another way of making "moving" pictures, but you need far less equipment than for the zoetrope.

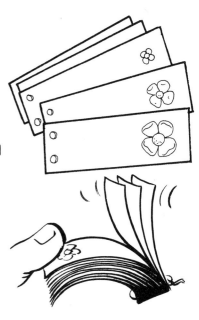

If you have a small thick notepad, then that, plus a pen or pencil, is all you need! If you haven't, you can easily make one. Cut up several sheets of paper into strips 10cm (4in) x 3cm (1¼in). You need at least 40 strips, but you can have as many as you like. Use a two-hole punch to make holes in the left-hand side of your strips and tie them together tightly with string.

Now make up a sequence of pictures, perhaps a flower opening and getting bigger, or a matchstick person putting up an umbrella or diving into the sea. Keep it very simple as you've got to draw it 40 times or more, making each picture just slightly different from the last to give that feeling of movement.

When you have drawn the last picture, flick over the pages and see the flower open or the hurdler jump. Amazing, isn't it? And you've just taken the first step to becoming a film animator!

The "turning wonder"

The most used picture on a "turning wonder" is of a parrot in a cage. The parrot is drawn on one side of a roundel and the cage on the other. When the roundel is spun, it appears as though the parrot is actually in the cage.

This ingenious little toy was first introduced to the public in the early years of the last century. Its real name is "thaumotrope", but "turning wonder" describes it perfectly.

First cut out two circles 7.5cm (3in) across, from a piece of thin cardboard. On one, draw a simple picture. For instance, you could draw a parrot in a cage or a circus acrobat balancing on a horse or a bird on a nest. Then transfer part of the design – the cage, horse or nest – to one side of the other roundel. Turn the roundel over by moving it away from you. Draw the remaining half of your picture on this side in exactly the same position as on your original design.

Attach a length of thin string to either side of the roundel, 15cm (6in) long. Holding the ends of the string in your right and left hands, spin the roundel until the string is twisted tightly. Then, stop spinning and pull at the ends of the string so that it begins to unwind. The roundel spins and the parrot is back in its cage.

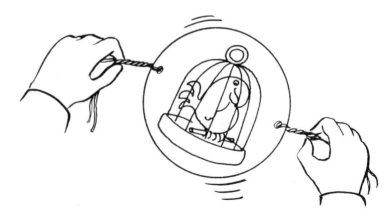

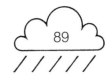

10 Creative crafts

We all like making things, but sometimes want to do something a little different to sewing the usual lavender bags or painting more greetings cards.

There are some ideas in this chapter that you may not have tried before. Some will provide unusual presents while others can be made just for the fun of it; and you will get a lot of pleasure from seeing the finished article on your wall or shelf.

The materials you will need should be readily available in the house, but read carefully through all the instructions before you start in case there is a vital ingredient that your household cannot supply. After all, someone may have just used up the last tube of glue!

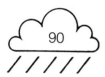

Seed and pasta pictures

What else can you do with pasta, lentils and beans apart from eat them? Why, make a picture, of course!

Ask your parents if you may have a selection from the jars and packets in the kitchen. Choose as many different types of each one as you can. Macaroni, spaghetti, pasta twists and shells, for example. Then select some beans and lentils that will add just the right subtle tints to your picture: red kidney beans, white haricot beans, green flageolet beans, yellow split peas and orange lentils. Pumpkin seeds and sunflower seeds can form part of the pattern or, if you are attempting a scene, they make good leaves and flowers, if arranged in a circular design.

Choose a nice bright cardboard as your base, perhaps blue, green or red, and select a glue that will stick the shapes firmly onto the card without sticking your fingers together as well.

Try to plan your picture first so that you have some idea what is going where. You may need tweezers to help you position all the pieces. It will probably be much easier to put glue on the cardboard and fill in small areas at a time rather than try to glue each shape down separately – a very messy business.

When you have finished, paint over your shapes with clear varnish to give it a nice shiny finish. You could use clear nail varnish if you haven't any other.

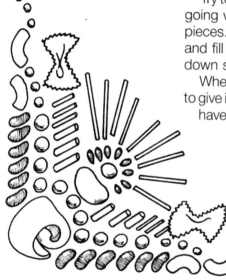

Don't just eat it, wear it!

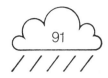

Now you've made your pasta picture, don't stop there, try your hand at pasta necklaces and bracelets too. Macaroni comes in different lengths and widths, some straight and some curved, so these are just the thing for a different kind of necklace. Paint or dye the macaroni before you start to thread it as a pale cream necklace isn't very attractive. Try a nice bright orange or blue.

There are many combinations of shapes you can experiment with and you will have fun making up your own designs. As well as threading single pieces of macaroni, why not glue two, three or four together? Choose some strong cotton thread and make your necklace long enough so that it will easily slip over your head.

Dried pumpkin and melon seeds can be used as well. Wash them and dye them in a cold water dye. They look most attractive threaded closely together on a long length of thread or elastic. Make a matching bracelet to go with your necklace. Thread it on thin elastic so that it easily stretches to go over your hand.

Why not try putting seeds and pasta together so that you have a macaroni and melon pip necklace? Sounds almost good enough to eat!

Rolled paperwork

Many, many years ago, when ladies had lots of spare time, they often passed many a pleasant hour engaged in rolled paperwork.

It is an unusual way of decorating box lids or even whole boxes and some very attractive cards can be made using a simple rolled paperwork design. It is not very difficult, but you need to take care as it is rather fiddly so you must also have the patience to take your time over it. You need lots of strips of narrow paper 8mm (¼in) wide – white will do as you can always paint the article when you have finished it.

Roll your paper several times around a pencil and glue the end down. If you want an oval or leaf shape, press the middle down slighty and pinch both ends. When you have prepared several shapes like this you can then plan your design.

You could stick some onto a home-made clay pendant or make an attractive birthday card by drawing in the stem of a flower and using oval shapes for the leaves and then cluster several circular shapes together for the flower head.

If you have an old can or box that is looking a bit shabby you could give it a coat of paint and then cover the lid and sides with rolled paper patterns.

To make it look really special, buy some gold or silver paper and use this cut and rolled into tiny shapes.

You may see examples of rolled paperwork in museums. Small boxes and tea-caddies, in particular, were often decorated in this way.

Paper flowers

Brighten up a dark winter's day by making some big gaudy paper flowers. You need some crêpe paper, some florists' wire or fuse wire and some thin canes or sticks.

Choose bright pinks, mauves, purples and oranges for a dazzling display. Cut out various different petal shapes like the ones illustrated. Glue the bases of eight petals together and group them around the top of one of the canes. Stick a second round of petals to the first to make a double flower then wind some thin wire around the base of the flower to attach it firmly to the stick.

Cut out strips of green paper 5cm (2in) wide and glue these around the cane to make it look more like the flower's stem. Make three or four long pointed leaves from the same green paper and glue these at intervals up the stem so that just the top half of the leaf flops back.

You can make flowers from just one shade or you can mix the papers up so that you have red and orange flowers, pink and mauve flowers and yellow and orange ones.

Make some really big ones that will stand in a tall vase on the floor or a table in a corner of the room. They will make an eye-catching display and, before you know it, you'll be making them for friends as well.

3-D pictures

The next time you go away or visit a big town, look out for postcards of the place that would make an attractive picture. Buy about four postcards, then on the next rainy day you can make a 3-D picture with them.

You need a fairly strong adhesive and a good pair of scissors. Decide which of the features in the postcard are the ones you want to stand out. It may be the mountains in the background, then a couple of trees and perhaps a cottage right in the foreground of the picture. In that case, cut out one mountain shape and stick it on to your base postcard, then two trees and stick those down one on top of the other and then three cottages. Gradually you will see the picture coming to life. You'll be able to remember it better now and see it again as it was when you visited the spot.

If you can find a small photograph frame or picture frame, put your postcard picture in this and hang it on your wall. If not, stick it to a larger piece of cardboard, attach some string to the back and then put it up in your bedroom.

Townscapes make good subjects too. Choose one with an imposing building in it, like a large church or cathedral or town hall.

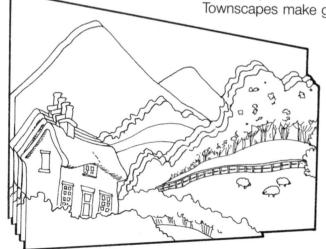

Noah's ark

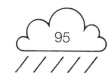
A Noah's ark is the very thing to make on a rainy day. You can get your animals to march on board where they'll be safe from the floods.

You need some thin cardboard, a paper adhesive and a pair of scissors. Copy the ark shape shown here, but make it much larger, of course; big enough, in fact, to take several pairs of animals.

Draw and cut out two identical ark shapes. Then put in the detail: windows, doors and roof tiles, as well as some decoration on the walls. Now cut a piece of paper as long as the ark and about 10cm (4in) wide. Fold back 1cm (½in) on either side of this paper strip and stick it to the two ark shapes so that it forms the deck.

All the animals are made in a similar way: two shapes are cut out and joined by a central piece of cardboard as shown in the illustration. This will ensure that they all stand up firmly. You can trace around the animal shapes here or copy them a little larger if you wish. Give the giraffe some big brown spots and paint the lion a soft yellow. Try to make the other animals look realistic too.

Then you can think up lots more creatures to go into the ark – farm animals, domestic animals, insects – and don't forget the worms and snails.

When all your animals are ready, cut out another rectangular shape for the gang-plank so that they can get onto the ark safely. And don't forget to make Mr and Mrs Noah, too.

Shoe-box dolls' house

It's great fun making tiny replicas of real things which is why a shoe-box dolls' house will provide hours of amusement.

The lid of the box will be the front of the house, which you could paint so that it resembles your own. The inside should be divided into a living room and a bedroom. Paint windows on the back wall and make little curtains to stick on. Then draw a fireplace in one side wall. Add in pictures and photographs to make it look really homely. Commemorative stamps stuck on the walls will look just like pictures. Go around the edge with a brown or black pencil so that it appears to be framed.

If you want to add on more rooms you can easily build an extension by glueing on another shoe-box.

By laying the shoe-box on its side you can make a bungalow or chalet-type house. Add as much detail on the outside of the house as possible to make it look really interesting. Have some climbing plants growing up around the doors and some hanging baskets and window boxes, too.

Gift wrap makes excellent wallpaper, expecially if you can find some with a small pattern on it. Small pieces of material will make rugs or carpets. Once you have started, you will also think up many more ideas of your own.

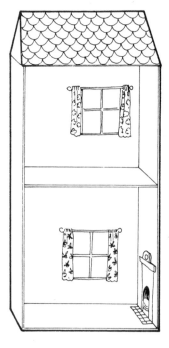

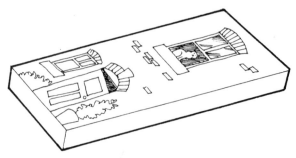

Dolls' house furniture

Matchbox furniture is just the right size for a shoe-box dolls' house but as matches are not used so much these days you may find it difficult to get enough to make a houseful of furniture.

Any small packets would do just as well or you may have to cut down larger ones. Cover all your furniture with white paper, then you can draw on the details, knobs for some drawers, handles for others.

Make a television with two slots in the side and the screen cut out so that you can push pieces of paper through with pictures drawn on. This way, you can change the channel whenever you feel like it.

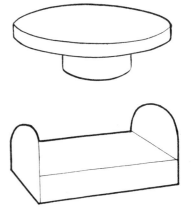

Once you have made your basic furniture, paint it and then make the furnishings: sheets, pillows and duvet covers for the beds and cushions for the chairs.

Then make some paper people for your house and add the family pets, a cat, dog and maybe even a goldfish bowl made from a bottle cap. Ornaments, vases, cups, plates and saucers can all be made from soft model clay. Cut out flowers from magazines, attach them to matchsticks or wire and put them in the vases. You may be able to find other illustrations in magazines that could be stuck onto the walls – a grandfather clock, for example, or maybe even a fine painting like the Mona Lisa!

Not bookmarks again!

Ah, but these are different. In any case, you can never have enough bookmarks. They are just like pens and pencils — no matter how many you have you can never find one when you need it. This is why they make excellent presents, too.

The usual ways of making bookmarks are by using pressed flowers, or making potato prints, leaf prints or perhaps even making cloth ones with embroidery on. So here is an idea for a bookmark that is a little different.

Think of some animals, birds or insects that you could draw so that they will look as though they are sitting on the top of the book.

On a piece of stiff cardboard draw a rectangle 5cm (2in) wide and 15cm (6in) long. Then on top of this draw an animal like the bush-baby here. If you give it a long tail curling round in front of it, then this can be cut out so that it slips over the page you are reading when you insert the bookmark. In the same way you could draw a monkey or an owl or eagle whose claws or talons clasp the top of the page. Draw a snail crawling along the top or a bee on a flower.

Then there's the boy here who is looking very relaxed, resting his arms along the top of the book. You could draw a face at both ends of the bookmark, one looking happy and one looking sad.

Look through some nature books for more ideas or perhaps history books and draw some characters from the past — Napoleon, Henry VIII or Abraham Lincoln. Florence Nightingale could hold her lamp over the page or King Arthur might rest his sword there.

11 Grow it indoors

If you enjoy gardening but find there are times when the weather is too bad for it, why not take up indoor gardening? It can be done at almost any time and you get year-round pleasure from it.

You will need quite a supply of potting compost plus some small pots and other containers. But plants, seeds and cuttings may be obtainable from other keen gardeners who live nearby and have more than they need. Often, if you show an interest, you will be given lots of tips and advice that can make your first attempt at indoor gardening an instant success.

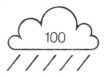

A topping garden

And that's exactly what you can make – a topping garden, or, to put it another way, a garden from tops.

Hang around the kitchen when a meal is being prepared and ask for the left-over carrot, parsnip, and turnip tops. Make sure they are really fresh vegetables as ones that have been stored at low temperatures may not be able to grow again.

Put your tops in a saucer or dish of water so that the water just covers the bottom part. Look at the water level each day and top up when necessary. Put your dish near a window so that your plant will get plenty of light. Within a few days you should be able to see little green shoots appearing. After a few weeks your carrot top will have sprouted a mass of delicate feathery foliage.

You can grow your tops upside down too. Cut about two inches from the top end of a carrot, scoop out a little of the inside and fill it with water. Push a knitting needle or skewer right through the carrot top, tie some string onto it and hang it up in a light, warm place. As long as you keep topping the water up you will soon see the green leaves appear. You can make it look even prettier by putting a few small cut flowers in the water.

The miniature garden

Miniature gardens are great fun to make and you can use almost any old container. If you are going to plant seeds, start in spring or late summer and buy ones that will grow into small plants. Choose your container and spread some small clean pebbles or gravel over the bottom. Then fill the tray with potting compost. Plant your seeds then sprinkle a little more potting compost over the top. Keep the soil moist but don't overwater it. Put the container in a light airy position.

If you are making a miniature garden using cut flowers, then some florists' foam will be useful.

Put some water into small dishes or mousse pots and fill them with moss or a combination of flowers and leaves so that the little containers are completely hidden. The flower heads of some weeds are very pretty and no one will mind if you pick a few to use in your miniature garden. They don't keep fresh for very long, but the beauty of this kind of garden is that you can replace flowers and leaves and things as they wither.

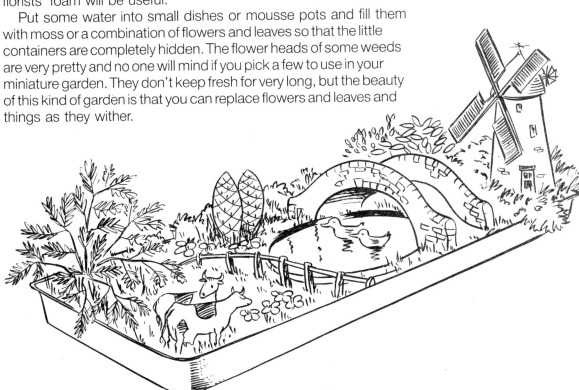

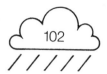
Growing things to eat

There are many food-producing plants that you can grow indoors in pots, or on a patio – plants like tomatoes, green beans and strawberries, for example. But if you want results in a hurry then go for the faster growing things like mustard and cress, bean shoots and herbs.

By adding mustard and cress to an egg or cheese sandwich, you instantly make it more tasty and interesting. And it is very easy to grow. A shallow polystyrene tray makes a good container, but you could just as easily use a bowl or saucer. Put two layers of damp absorbent paper into your container and scatter some cress seeds over one half of the paper. Cover with another sheet of paper or foil. Three days later, scatter mustard seeds on the other half and cover in the same way. Make sure you keep the paper moist, but not soaking wet. When you see the tiny shoots appearing you can remove the covering and keep them in a light or sunny spot. Your mustard and cress should be ready to cut and eat when the plants are 6-7cm (2½-3in) high.

Mung beans, better known as Chinese bean sprouts, are delicious to eat and grow very quickly. Wash them in a close mesh strainer under cold running water and soak overnight. In the morning wash the beans again and spread them out on a dish on some damp absorbent paper. Put the dish in a polythene bag and cover with newspaper or foil to keep out the light. Look at them each day to make sure the kitchen paper is still damp. If it is dry just add a very little water; too much and the bean shoots will turn furry and unpleasant.

They should be ready to eat in about a week's time.

Growing plants from cuttings

Some plants are so easy to grow you can almost watch them doing it. These tend to be the ones grown from cuttings. If you put the cuttings in water you will see the roots grow and when they look big and healthy you can transfer your plant to a pot.

There are stem cuttings, leaf cuttings and the spider plant that grows tiny little plants at the ends of its stem. These can be snipped off and put in water until the roots are about 2cm (1in) long, then they can be potted.

You can take leaf cuttings from several plants including African violet, begonia and gloxinia. Just cut off a nice healthy leaf and pop it into some potting compost. Water it and tie a polythene bag over the top. Keep it in a light warm place and you will soon see new young leaves appear.

Busy Lizzie (Impatiens) and Wandering Jew (Tradescantia) plants can be grown from stem cuttings. You need 15cm (6in) of stem from a healthy plant. Pop it in water until the roots start to grow, then pot it as before.

To grow an umbrella plant you will need a leaf end with 5cm (2in) of stem. Put the leaf end in some water and a root will grow from the middle. You can then pot the root and leaves in some potting compost leaving the stem showing above the earth. A new plant will begin to grow from the stem.

Plants from stones and seeds

Avocados, lychees and mangoes

The next time you have a fruit with a stone or pips in it why not try growing your own exotic plant? The stones of avocados, lychees and mangoes all grow into interesting plants and are grown in the same way.

Start the stone off in water or compost and place it somewhere dark and warm. During its early days it doesn't like the light. If your stone is in water, make sure the level always comes about halfway up the stone. If the stone should begin to turn green and slimy, rinse both it and the glass under running water before filling up with clean water again. The stone should split after about 3-6 weeks and shoots and roots will soon appear. When the shoot is about 2.5cm (1in) high, transfer the stone carefully to a 15cm (6in) pot and keep it in a warm, shady place where it will soon begin to grow quickly. As the plant grows larger you may have to repot it. In two or three years you could have a real giant of a plant.

Citrus fruits

The pips from oranges, lemons and grapefruit take much longer to grow so you will need to be patient. Put some broken pieces of pottery or little pebbles into small pots then fill with potting compost 7.5-10cm (3-4in) deep. Water the compost well and put 2-3 pips in each pot. Don't mix pips from different kinds of fruit as they grow at different rates. Stand the pots on a saucer in case any water seeps out, and keep in a dark, warm place. Shoots should begin to show

through in 1-2 months. When this happens, put the pot in a shady place for a day or two, then transfer it to a spot where it will get more light. Keep the compost moist, but do not overwater.

Peanuts

Have you ever thought of growing a peanut plant? It is one of the fastest growing plants so is ideal for those of you who like quick results. Buy the peanuts which are still in their shells and crack two or three so that the shells just split open. Plant the shells in wet compost, just pushed into the surface. Peanuts like to be both warm and wet so after planting your shells put the pot inside a polythene bag and keep it somewhere warm. After about 5 or 6 days the roots will start to grow and will push the peanut shell up out of the earth. At the end of another week you should see green leaves begin to sprout and within a month you will have a nice healthy plant.

A garden in a jar

To make a successful indoor garden that looks after itself, you first need to find a large glass jar or bottle that has a wide neck and a lid. By leaving the lid on the jar, no moisture will escape so it will be continually re-used.

Rinse the jar out thoroughly, then put a layer of washed gravel into the bottom. On top of this, sprinkle a layer of charcoal – barbecue charcoal will do fine – and then some potting compost so that you have now filled the bottom third of your jar. Unless the jar has a very wide neck you will not be able to get your hand inside, so tie a stick to an old teaspoon and use this as your spade. Carefully put your plants in one by one and use the spoon to press the compost down firmly around them. Your plants will need room to grow so don't be tempted to overfill your jar. Now trickle some water down the inside of the jar and put the lid on. You should not need to water your plants again for many months. The charcoal will absorb any excess moisture.

Now stand your terrarium – that's the proper name for a garden in a bottle – in a warm spot, out of direct sunlight and just wait for your plants to grow.

Cacti

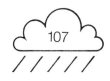

Cacti-growing is easy and fun. They store water in their stems so do not need to be watered as often as other plants. Their natural home is desert regions where it doesn't rain very often, so the plants are able to withstand quite dry conditions. You can raise cacti from seed, but it is a slow process. The plants themselves are not very expensive so if you bought a few small ones of different varieties you could watch them become fully grown plants.

Some cacti produce small "babies" so if you have friends with cacti of this type you could ask for one of these babies and plant it yourself. When you have removed it from the main plant, leave it to dry out for two or three days before repotting in damp compost. Water only lightly when the top of the soil has dried out.

During the summer, keep your cactus on a sunny windowsill and water every 3-4 days or so. You need not water your cactus at all in the winter unless it flowers during the cold months when it will need just a little water every 3-4 weeks.

You may have to wait a long time for your cactus to flower – some take as long as five years – but when flowers do appear they are often very spectacular and well worth waiting for.

Winter flowers

A pot of spring flowers is a lovely present to give at Christmas time, but you have to begin planning early. As soon as the leaves start falling off the trees in mid to late October, buy some bulbs and potting compost and set to work. You can choose from dozens of varieties of daffodils or tulips, snowdrops, hyacinths and crocus. Hyacinths are very popular as they have such a lovely scent.

Plant only one sort of bulb in a pot as different varieties grow at different rates. The bulb should be pushed deep into the compost so that just the tip is showing above the earth. Now put your pots of bulbs somewhere cool and dark until the shoots begin to show. Then they can be brought out into the warmth of a bedroom or living room and watered regularly to keep the compost moist.

Hyacinth bulbs are quite big and you can grow these in water without any soil at all. You need a glass jar with a neck just big enough for the hyacinth to sit in. Fill the jar so that the bottom of the bulb always sits in the water. You will then be able to watch the roots growing as well as the shoots and the flower.

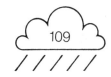

12 Preparing for a rainy day

It's a good idea to look ahead sometimes and think of things that can be done on rainy days that will need a little forward planning.

If you collect things, then save them for that rainy day so that you can sort them and label them. Stamps, postcards and photographs can be neatly stored until you can sit down and arrange them in an album.

If you can't bear to throw anything away, but must save every scrap of wrapping paper, cellophane wrappings, shiny foil from chocolate boxes and old Christmas or birthday cards, don't despair – there's a use for them all.

Just save them up for a rainy day which is sure to come sooner or later.

Collecting for an album

Stamps

If you already collect stamps then you will have a proper stamp album with the countries listed in alphabetical order. People mostly start by sticking in every stamp they possess, but then, as they realize the great variety of stamps available, they will often become more selective. You could have a whole album of stamps devoted to natural history, sport, transport or any other subject that takes your fancy.

Photographs

If you are a keen photographer, be selective about which photos go in your album. If they are too dark or too light, or someone's head is missing, then it's better not to include them. Photos such as these can be very boring to look at and friends will soon be less than enthusiastic when you ask if they would like to see your new photos!

... and the rest

There are, of course, many other things that people collect. Some make collections of cheese labels, stickers, cartoons, jokes, funny stories from newspapers and magazines, odd facts, sporting pictures, recipes, pop stars and so on. Why not choose one of the subjects here to start a new collection of your own?

Recycling greetings cards

Have you ever thought that you'd like to do something with all the birthday cards and Christmas cards you are given? Some are too pretty to throw away and some are too funny. If you don't actually want to re-use the cards again yourself there are lots of charities that would be very glad to have them. However, it is very easy to recycle them so that they can be used for a second time.

New cards from old
If you particularly like the picture on the front of the card, just cut it off and stick it on to stiff paper the same size as the original card. If you do this very carefully, no one will know that they have received a second-hand card. This is a good way of raising money as well, particularly at Christmas time. You could make cards in this way for family and friends and give the money you have saved to a charity.

Or you may want to use just part of a card, some flowers, say, or a dog or cat, because the background of the picture isn't very striking. All you have to do is cut around the part that you like and stick it on the front of some tinted card. This will make it a more noticeable feature of the card and you will have the satisfaction of having successfully re-used yet another one from your collection.

Using pressed flowers

This is a very popular pastime for both rainy and sunny days. On warm days in summer the flowers can be collected and carefully pressed and then used on the less pleasant days as a way of passing an enjoyable few hours. When you are collecting flowers, don't forget that leaves are very attractive as well, particularly as they turn red, brown, yellow and orange and drift down off the trees at the end of summer. They should be quite dry when picked or collected and it is better to do this in the middle of the day when they have dried out after being covered in early morning dew. Press them between two sheets of absorbent paper and leave them for four weeks or so between the pages of a large book or telephone directory.

Fat, fleshy flowers do not press well. It is far better to press their petals individually than to attempt to press the whole flower. Flowers with a single circle of petals press very well and should be opened up so that the whole flower can be seen clearly.

Flower pictures

If you are making a picture you can use either a very few flowers with the odd leaf or stem for a dramatic effect or you can cover nearly every part in a brilliant display of many different kinds of flowers. It is worth buying some clear sticky-back plastic to cover your picture with, as this will protect the flowers. It has to be applied very carefully or it will crinkle, so it is often better to ask someone else to help you do this.

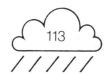

Cards and bookmarks
Cards and bookmarks should not be overcrowded with flowers, petals, leaves and grasses as the area in use is so small. It is much better to have just a few carefully chosen specimens that will look their best on a pale tinted background. Again, cover it in clear film for protection.

Flowers in albums
Another attractive way of using pressed flowers is to include them around photos or postcards in an album. Again, don't use too many, three or four flowers plus a few small leaves clustered around one corner is enough to make a very striking feature.

Calendars
If you have some dried flowers and grasses as well as pressed flowers, make an arrangement to stick on a calendar. You can buy little pocket calendars which you can stick below the arrangement.

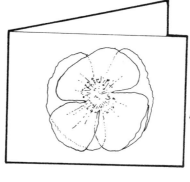

Collages

If you've been steadily collecting pictures from magazines to stick in an album and find that you now have rather a lot left over, why not make a collage with them? This is a way of using lots of different clippings to make a striking overall picture by grouping and overlapping them. Look through your collection to see if any of them have a linking theme and put them to one side. You may find you end up with several heaps and perhaps you could use a selection from two or three of them. Some clippings may have to be further reduced in size; a small area of one may be relevant to your picture while the rest of it is not. Cut away the background from some of them to give them a starker and more dramatic image.

Don't stick anything down until you have tried it out first. Get your sheet of paper ready and arrange your clippings on it. Stand back and take a good look at it. Does it all go together well? Or would certain things look better elsewhere? Move them all around until you are satisfied with your design. Then leave them all in position as you stick each one down making sure you overlap them correctly.

Mosaic pictures

The Greeks and Romans were very fond of making mosaic pictures for floor decorations and you may have seen some of the better examples in books about ancient Greece or Rome.

On a much more modest scale you can make mosaic pictures using all kinds of different scraps of paper. If you have carefully saved and pressed chocolate wrappers or cellophane or a particularly attractive wrapping paper, now's the time to look them all out and see how they can be used.

Draw the outline of a mosaic that you wish to make. Make it fairly simple and uncomplicated so that it is easily recognizable, like the butterfly in the illustration. Decide which pieces of paper are going where; you may have to cut up some of the larger pieces in your collection so that they fit more easily into the mosaic. If you are making the butterfly, start with the body and spread some glue just on that part. Then transfer the pieces you are using with a pair of tweezers so that you don't get too glued up. When the body is covered, gently press down all the pieces with your fingers to make sure they are stuck fast. Then you can cover another small area in the same way until the whole butterfly is finished.

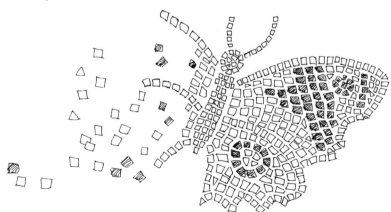

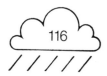

Things with shells

It's very difficult to go to the sea shore and not come back with a handful of shells. They look so attractive sparkling on the sand that we feel we just have to pick them up and take them home with us.

But when we get back home, what on earth do we do with them? Usually they end up in a forgotten heap at the back of a drawer. But they can be used to make pictures or decorate box lids, drawer fronts or door panels. You'll have to ask permission first before you start decorating the furniture, but if you can design some small and attractive arrangements your parents will probably say "yes".

You do need a strong adhesive as shells don't have many flat surfaces. Ladies used to spend many hours and days making beautiful shell pictures that resembled bunches of flowers. They used very small shells for petals and grouped them together to make the flower heads. You might try something simpler to start with like a flat geometric pattern or even an aerial view of a garden shouldn't be too difficult. When you are used to handling shells you will see ways of fitting them together to achieve the 3-D flower effect and you can progress to that a little later on.

Shells can also be used to decorate box lids which then look very attractive sitting on a dressing table or shelf and make a different kind of present for your mother or sister to keep necklaces and brooches in.

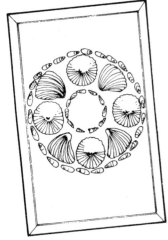